The Mystery of God

"...in the days of the sounding of the seventh
angel, when he is about to sound,
the mystery of God would be finished..."
Revelation 10:7

Tom Watts

All Scripture in this book is from *The New King James Version* of the Bible. Bold print was added by the author to emphasize a word, phrase, or thought.

First Printing 1997

ISBN 0-965-7533-0-1

Thomas R. Watts Ministries
P.O. Box 709
Broken Arrow, Oklahoma 74013-0709

Cover design: J. West Design, Tulsa
Editing and typesetting: M & B Graphics, Tulsa

Contents

Dedication

To my wife, Mary, whose love and support is enabling me to fulfill God's plan and purpose for my life.

Acknowledgments

Throughout my Bible school years, the teaching of Rev. Brian McCallum was a great inspiration to me. He encouraged me to seek the Teacher, the Holy Spirit, who unveils and reveals all prophetic Scripture. Thank you, Brian!

I'd like to thank my son and daughter-in-law, Brian and Kathy, for all their typing, and Gerry Reese and Glenda Kallenberger for their suggestions. I want to extend a special "thank you" to Linda Anderson for her help with structure and content.

Preface

To my brothers and sisters in Christ:

This is a Bible teaching book. More than that, it is a Bible study book. I want the Scripture itself to reveal the events of the end of this age. Therefore, much of the book is directly from Scripture, most of it from The Revelation of Jesus Christ. I believe that as you study this book, with the Holy Spirit as the Teacher, He will reveal and unveil His truth to your heart.

My hope is that this book will help us better understand the events at the end of this age. May we see the great harvest fields before us and the harvest yet to come!

If this book ministers grace and peace to your heart concerning the final events of this age, it has achieved one of its purposes. If it stirs you to fully surrender yourself to the plan and purpose of God for your life, then it has accomplished its other objective.

I'm looking forward to spending eternity with the family of God!

Tom Watts

Introduction

In the spring of 1977 at the age of forty, my wife, Mary, was born again. I witnessed a marvelous transformation in my wife! I wanted the same peace, joy, and love that I saw in Mary, so I asked Jesus into my heart too. That started a brand-new life for us — and for our family.

After I was baptized with the Holy Spirit in June 1979, God placed within me a desire to know what He is doing in the earth and to know what He *is going* to do. I read a lot of "prophetic" books and subscribed to several "prophetic" newsletters.

It is easy to get into a ditch studying any single area of God's activity, and I was no exception. I became convinced that in the fall of 1981, God was going to "rapture" or catch away His Church. The fall of 1981 came and went, and we were still here.

At the end of January 1982, I asked the Father, "When are You going to send Jesus to catch away Your family? I know that You won't reveal the day or the hour, but You said the Holy Spirit would show us things to come. So when are You going to 'rapture' Your Church?"

This book is the result of that question.

Chapter I

THE SIGN OF HIS COMING

In Matthew 24:3, Jesus' disciples asked Him, ". . .what will be **the sign** of Your coming, and of the end of the age?" Jesus told them of many things that would happen and then in verse 14 He answered their specific question: "And this gospel of the kingdom will be preached in **all** the world as a witness to **all** the nations, and **then** the **end** will come."

The sign, or witness, of Jesus' coming at the end of this age is that the Gospel of the Kingdom will be preached in **all** the world, as a witness to **all** the nations!

First Timothy 2:3 and 4 tells us, ". . .God our Savior, who desires all men to be saved and to come to the knowledge of the truth." James 5:7 says, "Therefore be patient, brethren, until the coming of the Lord. See how the farmer waits for the precious fruit of the earth, waiting patiently for it until it receives the early and latter rain."

Second Peter 3:9 tells us, "The Lord is not slack concerning His promise, as some count slackness, but is longsuffering toward us, not willing that any should perish but that all should come to repentance."

Jesus will come for His Church! There is no doubt about that! But He will not come until the Gospel of the

Kingdom has been preached in **all** the world as a witness or sign to **all** the nations! Will Jesus come this year (1997)? No. Why not? Because we have many unreached people upon the earth who have never yet heard the Gospel, let alone seen it demonstrated.

The Gospel of the Kingdom

The Gospel of the Kingdom is the truth of God's Word being preached, taught, and demonstrated. The Gospel is more than a Sunday sermon, a Gospel tract, or a Christian radio or TV program. The Gospel of the Kingdom is God's people preaching, teaching, demonstrating, and living God's truth under the direction and anointing of the Holy Spirit. As this is done throughout the earth, Jesus will be lifted up and will draw all mankind to Himself (John 12:32). All who have open hearts will be saved. Whoever calls upon the Name of the Lord Jesus will be saved (Rom. 10:13)!

During His three and a half years of ministry, Jesus demonstrated the Gospel of the Kingdom. He was anointed with the Holy Spirit and power, and went about doing good and healing all who were oppressed by the devil (Acts 10:38). Jesus went about all the cities and villages, teaching in their synagogues, preaching the Gospel of the Kingdom and healing every sickness and every disease among the people (Matt. 9:35). As He did this, He continually announced that the Kingdom of God was among the people.

Jesus did nothing on His own but was totally submitted to His Heavenly Father. The following passages from the Gospel of John illustrate that fact.

JOHN 5:19,30
19 "...the Son can do nothing of Himself, but what He sees the Father do....
30 "I can of Myself do nothing. As I hear, I judge; and My judgment is righteous, because I do not seek My own will but the will of the Father who sent Me."

JOHN 7:16
16 "...My doctrine is not Mine, but His who sent Me."

JOHN 12:49,50
49 "For I have not spoken on My own authority; but the Father who sent Me gave Me a command, what I should say and what I should speak.
50 "...Therefore, whatever I speak, just as the Father has told Me, so I speak."

JOHN 14:10,11
10 "Do you not believe that I am in the Father, and the Father in Me? The words that I speak to you I do not speak on My own authority; but the Father who dwells in Me does the works.
11 "Believe Me that I am in the Father and the Father in Me, or else believe Me for the sake of the works themselves."

JOHN 10:37,38
37 "If I do not do the works of My Father, do not believe Me;
38 "but if I do, though you do not believe Me, believe the works, that you may know and believe that the Father is in Me, and I in Him."

We are the **Body** of Christ! **We**, the born-again ones, are Christ in the earth! We are **not** God, but we are the sons of God! We are Christ's Body in the earth. Jesus, our Head, is seated at the right hand of the Father. When Jesus left the earth, He told us, His Body, that all authority in Heaven and earth had been given to Him. Then His disciples, and that includes us today, were to go and make disciples of **all** the nations.

We are to preach and teach the truth of God. We are to walk in the power of the Holy Spirit. We are to cast out demons. We are to lay hands on the sick. We are to do the works of Jesus (John 14:12). We are to present the Gospel of the Kingdom just as Jesus presented it during His time of ministry on the earth!

If we are going to be successful in this Great Commission that Jesus gave us, then we must be totally submitted to His will. We must not speak **our** words, but **His** words. We must not do **our** works, but **His** works. Like Jesus, we must teach, preach, and demonstrate the manifestation of the Kingdom of God among us.

To complete the Great Commission, we must operate under the leadership and with the anointing of the Holy Spirit. "For as many as are led by the Spirit of God, these are sons of God" (Rom. 8:14). **Sons** who are led by the Spirit do the work of their Father, while **children** tend to just play around and mess things up. We need to dedicate ourselves to seek and serve God! We must obey His Word and be led by His Spirit.

Furthermore, we must be cautious not to do the works assigned to a fellow servant or to intrude on another servant's office or calling. Such was the case with King Saul, and it cost him the anointing and, eventually, the Kingdom (I Sam. 13:8-15). In this final move of God, it will take every believer standing in his own unique calling and purpose to complete the Father's business.

Jesus will come for us when we have preached, taught, and **demonstrated** the Gospel of the Kingdom in **all** the world as a sign to **all** the nations! Therefore, let us get about our Father's business!

Our Father's Business

A lot of us haven't taken the time to think about our Father's business. What is our Heavenly Father doing? Well, He's gathering a family for Himself. Ever since Adam's fall in the Garden, our Heavenly Father has been unfolding His plan tc redeem mankind back to Himself.

What a great peace and joy we experience when we are born again and united with our Heavenly Father, by the indwelling presence of the Holy Spirit, through our faith in the Lord Jesus Christ. Our Heavenly Father wants every single person on the face of this earth to have the opportunity to come into that relationship with Him. He is not willing that any should perish but that all should come to repentance (II Peter 3:9)!

Our Father is not gathering gold or silver; He's gathering His family. All that He will get out of this age is a family for Himself! God loves mankind, and He was willing to spend several thousand years making a way for us to be reunited with Him. He has spent the last two thousand years drawing us to Himself through Jesus. He uses the family members that are here upon the earth as vessels to carry out His plan. It is through us that He pours out His love, His Word, and His power upon those people who do not yet have a relationship with Him.

That's our Father's business, and we need to get about our Father's business. When we've completed His business, our Father will send Jesus to bring us home!

Chapter II

TWO BLOODS

The Blood of the Righteous

When He opened the fifth seal, I saw under the altar the souls of those who had been slain for the word of God and for the testimony which they held.

*And they cried with a loud voice, saying, "How long, O Lord, holy and true, until You **judge** and **avenge our blood** on those who dwell on the earth?"*

Then a white robe was given to each of them; and it was said to them that they should rest a little while longer, until both the number of their fellow servants and their brethren, who would be killed as they were, was completed.

— Revelation 6:9-11

The blood of the righteous has a voice, and it calls out to God from the earth. It is the life of the flesh, and when it is spilled unjustly, it cries out to God for justice and vengeance.

God hears the blood of the righteous which cries to Him from the earth. "Then the Lord said to Cain, 'Where is Abel your brother?' He said, 'I do not know. Am I my brother's keeper?' And He said, 'What have you done? The **voice** of your brother's **blood** cries out to Me from the ground'" (Gen. 4:9,10).

Yes, the blood of the righteous has a voice which cries out to God. It cries for justice and vengeance. During the past 2,000 years, untold millions of righteous people who served God have been slain for the Word of God and for the testimony which they held. The testimony they held was the testimony of Jesus.

God will answer that blood, because He is a just and fair God. When will He answer that blood? "...they should rest a little while longer, until both the **number** of their fellow servants and their brethren, who would be killed as they were, was **completed**" (Rev. 6:11). God will not answer the voice of the blood of the righteous until it is time to call His family home. Do you realize that more Christians have been killed in this century for the Word of God and for their testimony than in all the previous centuries dating back to Christ? This blood will be answered, but not until after the most powerful blood has been answered!

The Blood of Jesus

The voice of the blood of the righteous cries to God from the earth for justice and vengeance. But the **blood** of **Jesus** speaks to God from the altar of Heaven, and it speaks **better things** than the blood of Abel (Heb. 12:24)! The blood of Jesus speaks mercy, grace, forgiveness, salvation, redemption, cleansing, healing, and release from all bondage! The blood of Jesus speaks from Heaven for the spirits of all mankind.

Just as our blood gives life to our outward man (our body), so the blood of Jesus gives *eternal* life to our inward man (our spirit). The blood of Jesus was shed for all mankind so that whosoever would call on the Name of the Lord Jesus would be saved and spend eternity with the God of Heaven. The only alternative for man is to die physically without Jesus. Then his inward man will spend eternity in the fires of hell, paying for his own sins, because he didn't receive God's Substitute for his sins, Jesus the Savior.

God the Father is patiently waiting for the precious fruit of the earth. He will not answer the blood of the righteous until every person on the face of the earth has had an opportunity to receive Jesus. The blood of Jesus will be answered first!

Symbolism

The Revelation of Jesus Christ is primarily a prophetic Book. Prophetic Scripture contains more symbolic language than is found in other Scripture. The reason for symbolism in this type of Scripture is that prophetic Scripture is for God's people, a people who have the Holy Spirit active in their lives. The Holy Spirit wrote all Scripture, and He reveals and teaches all Scripture (John 14:17,26; 16:13). God wants His people, His co-laborers, to know what He is doing now and what He will be doing in the future. Prophetic Scripture requires much studying, meditating, and relying upon the Holy Spirit to reveal its truths.

In Bible school, my eschatology teacher said, "A good general guide to follow when studying prophetic

Scripture is: If it makes plain sense, take the plain sense. If it doesn't make plain sense, then look for the symbolism."

This is excellent advice. Some prophetic Scripture may make plain sense and still have a symbolic meaning. Often, prophetic Scripture has a double meaning, both natural and spiritual. For example, when prophetic Scripture is talking about a harvest of wheat, barley, grapes, and so forth, it may very well mean exactly that. However, God's spiritual harvest is always **souls**! God harvests only people. He brings them into a spiritual life and a relationship with Him. Or, in the case of those who reject Him, they are brought into physical death and spiritual death, where their spirit, soul, and body are separated from God.

God uses the **same symbols throughout Scripture**; they don't change their meanings. God never changes. He is the same yesterday, today, and forever (Heb. 13:8). Therefore, if we want to know what something symbolizes, we need to see how God used it — and what it refers to — in other parts of the Bible.

The Revelation of Jesus Christ is written to the servants of Jesus (Rev. 1:1). It will bring blessing to all who read, hear, and do what it says (Rev. 1:3). Its purpose is to minister grace and peace (Rev. 1:4) and to reveal or unveil the ministry of Jesus Christ. It is written to the seven churches that were in Asia at the time of its writing (Rev. 1:4,11).

The number seven is used 87 times in the New Testament, 53 of these are in this final Book. Symbolically, the number seven represents fullness, completion, or being complete. The seven churches are representative of the complete Church throughout the complete Church Age. What we find written to them can apply to the entire Church and to any local church body that exists today.

In the Scripture, "white" always symbolizes righteousness and purity. If someone has a white robe or rides a white horse, he is a "good guy."

This basic understanding of symbolism in Scripture will help you grasp the plan of God for man in the end of the age.

Chapter III

TWO HARVESTS

In the last chapter, we discussed two bloods — the blood of the righteous and the blood of Jesus. The result of those two bloods' speaking to God will be two harvests of people.

The **first**, the **harvest** of the **righteous**, started more than 1,900 years ago when the blood of Jesus was placed upon the altar in Heaven. It will reap its greatest number of people during the huge, end-of-the-age harvest.

The **second**, in response to the blood of the righteous, will be a **harvest** of the **wicked** who remain upon the earth. Its purpose will be to judge and avenge the blood of the righteous, which has been unjustly shed.

These two harvests, the second immediately following the first, are pictured in Revelation 14.

REVELATION 14:14-16
14 Then I looked, and behold, a white cloud, and on the cloud sat One like the Son of Man, having on His head a golden crown, and in His hand a sharp sickle.
15 And another angel came out of the temple, crying with a loud voice to Him who sat on the cloud, "Thrust in Your sickle and reap, for the time has come for You to reap, for the harvest of the earth is ripe."
16 So He who sat on the cloud thrust in His sickle ON the earth, and the earth was reaped.

This is a picture of Jesus Christ, harvesting souls from the earth. Notice that He is doing the harvesting **on** the earth. We are His Body, and He harvests through us, by the Word of God and the power of the Holy Spirit.

REVELATION 14:17-19
17 Then another angel came out of the temple which is in heaven, he also having a sharp sickle.
18 And another angel came out from the altar, who had power over fire, and he cried with a loud cry to him who had the sharp sickle, saying, "Thrust in your sharp sickle and gather the clusters of the vine of the earth, for her grapes are fully ripe."
19 So the angel thrust his sickle INTO the earth and gathered the vine of the earth, and threw it into the great winepress of the wrath of God.

This second harvest is done by angels in response to the blood which the angel gathers from the vine **within** the earth. It is the righteous blood which cries for justice and vengeance.

The second harvest is God's wrath being poured out upon the wicked, who reject the blood of Jesus and blaspheme His Name.

Answering the Blood of the Lamb —
Harvesting the Righteous

The result of the Gospel of the Kingdom being preached — through the Word of God and demonstrated by the works of the Holy Spirit in **all** the world as a sign to **all** the nations — will be the greatest harvest of souls coming to Jesus in the history of mankind! It will be the largest harvest recorded in the Bible — so large it cannot be counted!

REVELATION 7:9,13,14
9 After these things I looked, and behold, a great multitude which NO ONE COULD NUMBER, of all nations, tribes, peoples, and tongues, standing before the throne and before the Lamb, clothed with white robes. . . .
13 . . . "Who are these arrayed in white robes, and where did they come from?"
14 . . . "These are the ones who come out of the GREAT TRIBULATION, and washed their robes and made them white in the blood of the Lamb."

Here we see a picture of the great harvest at the end of this age — a harvest that comes from every **nation, family, race,** and **ethnic group** on the face of the earth! A harvest so large it cannot be counted! It is a huge multitude coming to Jesus **during** the **Great Tribulation!**

Most of us in the Body of Christ have had a very distorted picture of the Great Tribulation.

For some reason, we've thought that the devil would be in charge, not God. Shame on us for exalting the power of a fallen angel over the power of Almighty God! Instead of focusing on what God will be doing in this period, we have instead emphasized the works of Satan.

But God's power has not been diminished! *It never will!* God is simply waiting for a people, a Church, a body upon this earth, who will set their hearts and minds to serve Him; have knowledge of and faith in His

Word; and open themselves to the leadership and power of the Holy Spirit. That body is emerging all over the earth!

It is through this body of believers that God is pouring out His love, truth, and power in every nation of the earth, so that all peoples can hear and see the Gospel. God is not winding down; He is cranking up!

Answering the Blood of the Righteous — Harvesting the Wicked

There will come a time when the Gospel of the Kingdom will have been preached, taught, and demonstrated in the whole world; a time when God's family encompasses every nation, family, race, and ethnic group on the face of the earth; a time when every open heart has received Jesus.

At that time, all who are not in God's family will be resisters of God. Some will be haters and mockers of God. Others will have a form of godliness, but will deny the power of God and the truth of salvation.

As the response to the voice of the blood of Jesus decreases, the voice of the blood of the righteous will increase. God will answer the voice of the blood of the righteous and pour out His wrath upon the ungodly. He will answer the blood of His children who were slain for the Word of God and for their testimony. It will be a time of great wrath as God spills upon the earth unrighteous blood to avenge the blood of His children who were unjustly killed.

REVELATION 14:19,20
19 So the angel thrust his sickle into the earth and gathered the vine of the earth, and threw it into the great winepress of the wrath of God.
20 And the winepress was trampled outside the city, and blood came out of the winepress, up to the horses' bridles, for one thousand six hundred furlongs.

When the angel thrusts his sickle **into** the earth, he pulls up the vine of the earth and presses out the measure of the blood of the righteous, crying for justice and vengeance. It is this huge volume of blood, crying out to God, which results in God's wrath being poured out upon the wicked and upon the world system.

This is a judgment of God on flesh, in response to the voice of the blood, which was the life of the flesh of His children. I believe it will be avenged with an equal amount of blood, spilled from those who remain upon the earth as God pours out His wrath.

During most of this horrible time upon the earth, we will be in Heaven, standing before the reward seat of Christ (*see* Chapter XIV of this book).

Chapter IV

OVERVIEW OF
THE GREAT TRIBULATION

In the last chapter, we saw that the **largest harvest of souls recorded** in the **Bible** comes during the **Great Tribulation**. It comes from every nation, race, family, and ethnic group on the face of the earth! It is the great harvest at the end of this age.

As believers, we need to allow the Holy Spirit to teach us the truth concerning the Great Tribulation, and allow His Word to minister grace and peace to our hearts. When a believer reads any part of the Bible, it should minister grace and peace; it should produce faith, not fear! If we are receiving fear from any part of the Bible, then we are reading it wrong! We need to ask the Holy Spirit to teach us the truth so that faith will arise, and peace will dominate our hearts. The Book of The Revelation of Jesus Christ should do exactly the same!

We need to see the period of the Great Tribulation as a time of harvest. The first part of this period is described in the period of the first two trumpets. It is a time of the final, great harvest, of people coming to Jesus! It is a huge, **swift** and **supernatural** harvest of the entire earth. People will come to Jesus from every nation, tribe, people, and tongue upon the face of the earth. It is the time when the Jews will come to Jesus, the Arabs will come to Jesus. Millions, and I believe billions, of people will come to Jesus!

The Great Tribulation will **also** be a time of **judgment** as we move rapidly to the end. The period of the seven trumpets will see increased judgments as the harvest starts to decrease.

During the final three trumpets, God's judgment will progress to His wrath. Throughout history, man (and even whole denominations) have been inclined to focus on just one aspect of God's nature — either His judgment or His mercy. The truth is, God is both! He is a God of judgment and a God of mercy. Paul admonished the Church at Rome never to presume upon God's nature but that His goodness was meant to lead them to repentance (Rom. 2:4). Our duty, then, as believers is to teach the truth that God is love (and mercy), but when man lives contrary to His Word, judgment ensues.

The Revelation of Jesus Christ is an exciting study of God's character, because it portrays both elements of His nature. God is truly the central character!

The last part of the Great Tribulation is detailed in the seven bowls of God's wrath. It will be a time to complete the harvesting of the wicked and judging the world system; a time of great wrath; a time when God's family is gone from the earth, and the earth is under the sway of the spirit of antichrist (however, the Holy Spirit will still be here, and people can be saved). It will be a horrible time to be upon this earth! We should pray that no stubborn person will resist the love and power of God during the final great harvest! We'll look at the Great Tribulation in more detail as this book progresses.

Chapter V

BRETHREN
OR FELLOW SERVANT?

When He opened the fifth seal, I saw under the altar the souls of those who had been slain for the word of God and for the testimony which they held.

And they cried with a loud voice, saying, "How long, O Lord, holy and true, until You judge and avenge our blood on those who dwell on the earth?"

*Then a white robe was given to each of them; and it was said to them that they should rest a little while longer, until both the number of their **fellow servants** and their **brethren**, who would be killed as they were, was completed.*

— Revelation 6:9-11

In this passage of Scripture, we see two categories of Christians: **brethren** and **fellow servants**. We can see from this passage that they both get to Heaven; however, there is a marked difference between the two.

Brethren

The moment a person receives Jesus Christ into his heart, that person is born again. He or she enters the family of God and becomes a brother or sister with all the other members of God's family, whether in

Heaven or here upon the earth. That person is a brother, a born-again member of God's family.

That happened to my wife, Mary, and me in 1977. Prior to that point in my life, I was doing "my thing." I was following the plan and the purpose that Tom Watts had established for his life. I was a successful dentist and orthodontic specialist on a career path in the U. S. Army. I was prospering in my chosen career path and in the things the world system promotes. Then I became one of the brethren in the Body of Christ but was still following my own plan and purpose for my life. The fact that I needed to be about my Father's business was foreign to my thinking.

As I spent more time reading my Bible, talking with God, reading Christian books, and fellowshipping with other believers, I began to grow spiritually. I could see that God had a plan and a purpose for my life. As I thought about what God might have for me, I was overcome with fear. I was afraid that God would send me to some far-off jungle as a missionary dentist, and I would have to leave my family!

However, as I continued to grow spiritually, I learned that those negative, fearful thoughts came from the enemy, not God! I also learned that God will never send you anywhere that He doesn't first put within you a great desire to be there. And when you arrive, wherever it might be, you couldn't be happier or more fulfilled in any other place, no matter what the conditions might be.

Fellow Servant

There came a time in Mary's and my life — over a period of about six months, from the fall of 1979 to the spring of 1980 — when we decided to turn our lives over totally to the direction of the Lord. We made the decision that not our will, but His will, should be accomplished through our lives. We made the decision to leave all of our plans behind and to only follow Him. We became **fellow servants** of the Lord. Another word for fellow servant is **disciple**.

"Then Jesus said to His disciples, 'If anyone desires to come after Me, let him deny himself, and take up his cross, and follow Me'" (Matt. 16:24).

My cross is the distinctive will of God for my life. It is following God's plan and His purpose for my life. God's will for Jesus took Him to **the** Cross. His will for me will take me some other place. However, I could never know His will for my life until I first deny myself and choose to follow Him!

"Then He [Jesus] said to them all, 'If anyone desires to come after Me, let him deny himself, and take up his cross **daily**, and follow Me'" (Luke 9:23). Unfortunately, it is easy to start out serving the Lord and end up serving self again. We've seen the example of numerous ministers and ministries that fell in the past decade. They probably started out following God but eventually strayed from God's plan to their own plan.

It's easy to do. Many things are good, but that doesn't mean they are God's direction for my life. We are each individual members of the Body and we are not all called to do the same things! That is why Jesus tells us in Luke to take up our cross **daily**. We must each seek, and continue to seek, His will for our life.

God's road is narrow, but it is a road! As we walk on His road on a daily basis, it will be a much easier walk than when we stumble off into the ditch or follow some connecting road where a sign says, "This is a good road."

From Brother to Fellow Servant

When we are born again and we become freed from the bondage of sin and Satan, we fall in love with Jesus. As we grow in that love and in the knowledge of Him, we should give our lives back to Him and become His servants forever. We should set aside our self-made plan and ask Him for His heavenly made plan for our lives.

Mary and I have been blessed beyond any measure I can describe since we turned our lives over to Him! God has nothing but good in His plan for us!

I am not saying we won't have the struggles of life with which we must deal. I *am* saying that if we serve God with our whole heart, we will walk under His mighty hand of protection and provision. Believe me, when God is protecting and providing, life is far above all we can ask or think!

If you're not yet a fellow servant of the Lord, let me encourage you to turn your whole life over to Him. He needs every one of us during this great end-of-the-age harvest! And besides that, in just a few short years when you stand before the reward seat of Christ in Heaven, you will be **very glad** you did!

Chapter VI

TWO BOOKS

Just as there are two bloods, and two harvests in response to the voice of those bloods, there are also two books. These books reveal God's response to the voice of each blood.

The Large Book (Scroll)

REVELATION 5:1-9

1   And I saw in the right hand of Him who sat on the throne a scroll written inside and on the back, sealed with seven seals.

2   Then I saw a strong angel proclaiming with a loud voice, "Who is worthy to open the scroll and to loose its seals?"

3   And no one in heaven or on the earth or under the earth was able to open the scroll, or to look at it.

4   So I wept much, because no one was found worthy to open and read the scroll, or to look at it.

5   But one of the elders said to me, "Do not weep. Behold, the Lion of the tribe of Judah, the Root of David, has prevailed to open the scroll and to loose its seven seals."

6   And I looked, and behold, in the midst of the throne and of the four living creatures, and in the midst of the elders, stood a Lamb as though it had been slain, having seven horns and seven eyes, which are the seven Spirits of God sent out into all the earth.

7   Then He came and took the scroll out of the right
hand of Him who sat on the throne.
8   Now when He had taken the scroll, the four living
creatures and the twenty-four elders fell down before
the Lamb, each having a harp, and golden bowls full of
incense, which are the prayers of the saints.
9   And they sang a new song, saying: "You are worthy
to take the scroll, and to open its seals; for You were
slain, and have redeemed us to God by Your blood out
of every tribe and tongue and people and nation."

Of all those on earth and in Heaven, only one was
found worthy to open the seals of this large scroll. That
One was the Lord Jesus Christ! This large scroll is the
story of answering the blood of Jesus. It is the story of
the **redemption** of mankind. It starts when the first
seal is opened, and we see the Lord working by Himself
when He comes forth conquering. He defeats sin and
Satan by Himself!

As the first seal is opened and the scroll is unrolled,
we see Jesus all alone doing His perfect, righteous, and
victorious work. Then He leaves the earth for Heaven
and gives His authority, His Word, and His Spirit to the
born-again ones of the earth. This Church, which is His
Body, starts out all right but progressively falls back
into sin, unbelief, disobedience, and the traditions of
men.

By the time the fourth seal is opened, we see
revealed the depth of the Dark Ages when His Church
had become no more than an infighting religious organi-
zation, controlled by the devil and doing the devil's
work. The Word of God, wherein is resident the life and

power of God, had been totally withdrawn from men and women. It was literally chained to the pulpit, read only on Sunday and in a language that was not understood by the common man. It was a capital offense, punishable by death, for any common person to have any part of the Bible in his possession. In its place had been substituted numerous rituals, far removed from the truth of God's Word.

As the fifth seal is opened, the light of God's Word starts to touch the hearts of a few men who had access to the Bible. A period called the Reformation began. During this period, Johann Gutenberg invented the moveable type printing press. Copies of the Holy Scriptures in the common language of man soon became available. Although the persecution of these few believers intensified, it only fanned the flames of revival.

This Reformation, which started with the Waldensian movement of Peter Waldo in 1175 AD, has continued until this very day. The end of the last century saw a fresh outpouring of the Holy Spirit and a new anointing and revival of the Church, Christ's **Body** in the earth. This present-day revival will continue to grow, because it is built upon spiritual understanding of the written Word of God so that we might grow into the unified and obedient **Body** of the Living Word and Head of the Church, Jesus Christ.

Finally, when the seventh seal is opened, the final period of this age is revealed. This last seal initiates the seven trumpets of harvest, the final great harvests of mankind. First, the harvest of the righteous in response to the blood of Jesus. Second, the harvest of the wicked in response to the blood of the righteous.

The last, or seventh trumpet, then reveals the seven bowls for the completion of God's wrath. It is the time when God finishes answering the blood of the righteous and judges mystery Babylon the Great.

The Little Book

REVELATION 10:1-11
1 I saw still another mighty angel coming down from heaven, clothed with a cloud. And a rainbow was on his head, his face was like the sun, and his feet like pillars of fire.
2 He had a little book open in his hand. And he set his right foot on the sea and his left foot on the land,
3 and cried with a loud voice, as when a lion roars. When he cried out, seven thunders uttered their voices.
4 Now when the seven thunders uttered their voices, I was about to write; but I heard a voice from heaven saying to me, "Seal up the things which the seven thunders uttered, and do not write them."
5 The angel whom I saw standing on the sea and on the land raised up his hand to heaven
6 and swore by Him who lives forever and ever, who created heaven and the things that are in it, the earth and the things that are in it, and the sea and the things that are in it, that there should be delay no longer,
7 but in the days of the sounding of the seventh angel, when he is about to sound, the mystery of God would be finished, as He declared to His servants the prophets.
8 Then the voice which I heard from heaven spoke to me again and said, "Go, take the little book which is

open in the hand of the angel who stands on the sea and on the earth."
9 So I went to the angel and said to him, "Give me the little book." And he said to me, "Take and eat it; and it will make your stomach bitter, but it will be as sweet as honey in your mouth."
10 Then I took the little book out of the angel's hand and ate it, and it was as sweet as honey in my mouth. But when I had eaten it, my stomach became bitter.
11 And he said to me, "You must prophesy again about many peoples, nations, tongues, and kings."

This little book, which the angel gave to John, reveals the response of God to the blood of the righteous, shed for the Word of God and for the testimony of Jesus. It tells of God's wrath on the wicked in response to that blood.

When John ate the little book, it was sweet as honey in his mouth (v. 10). The **mouth symbolizes** our **outward man**, our flesh. The flesh still has that old nature in it. The flesh says, "An eye for an eye and a tooth for a tooth!" The flesh says, "Get 'em God; they deserve Your wrath!" But the book was bitter to John's stomach. The **stomach symbolizes** our **inward man**.

The inward man is a born-again spirit. The inward man is washed in the blood of the Lamb. The inward man cries, "Save them, God!" The inward man cannot stand to see anyone, no matter how bad they have been, go to hell! God's wrath is bitter to our born-again spirit, our inward man.

Remember that prophetic Scripture contains more symbolic language than is found in other Scripture, because prophetic Scripture is for God's people — people who have the Holy Spirit active in their lives.

Chapter VII

THREE PEOPLES

Several years ago, one of my favorite Bible teachers related the following story. She was at her kitchen sink washing dishes. The Lord spoke to her heart and gave her a scripture, First Corinthians 10:32. He told her this scripture would help keep her end-time doctrine straight. It has been a help to me ever since I heard her share it. "Give no offense, either to the **Jews** or to the **Greeks** or to the **church** of God" (I Cor. 10:32).

These are the three groups of people in the earth with whom God is dealing — the Jews, the Greeks, and the Church of God.

The Jews

God has been dealing with the Jews for several thousand years. He brought them forth as a people from the loins of Abraham. God fully intends to demonstrate the Gospel of the Kingdom to them in a very powerful way during the end of this age (*see* Chapter IX of this book). In prophetic Scripture, the Jews are referred to as the **earth**.

The Church of God

The Church of God, His Body on the earth, is the vessel through whom God flows. He must mold, shape, and purify that vessel before He can effectively use it.

Therefore, God has, is, and will continue to deal strongly with His Body, the Church of God. He deals with us as individuals, as local church bodies, and as the whole Church Body upon the earth.

The Greeks (The Nations)

The Greeks, or the nations, are all those peoples upon the earth who do not belong to the Church or who are not Jews. In prophetic Scripture, these nations are symbolically referred to as the **sea**. They are the focal point of the harvest, because, along with the Jews, God will have His Church preach, teach, and demonstrate the Gospel of the Kingdom to every creature. Looking at this task from a natural standpoint, it is impossible. Fortunately, God works in the supernatural, and nothing is impossible with God! He will not only accomplish it; He'll do it in a very short time!

Darkness

ROMANS 1:18-32
18 For the wrath of God is revealed from heaven against all ungodliness and unrighteousness of men, who suppress the truth in unrighteousness,
19 because what may be known of God is manifest in them, for God has shown it to them.
20 For since the creation of the world His invisible attributes are clearly seen, being understood by the things that are made, even His eternal power and Godhead, so that they are without excuse,
21 because, although they knew God, they did not glorify Him as God, nor were thankful, but became futile in their thoughts, and their foolish HEARTS were

DARKENED.
22 Professing to be wise, they became fools,
23 and changed the glory of the incorruptible God
into an image made like corruptible man—and birds
and four-footed animals and creeping things.
24 Therefore God also gave them up to uncleanness,
in the lusts of their hearts, to dishonor their bodies
among themselves,
25 who EXCHANGED the TRUTH of God for the LIE,
and worshiped and served the creature rather than
the Creator, who is blessed forever. Amen.
26 For this reason God gave them up to vile passions.
For even their women exchanged the natural use for
what is against nature.
27 Likewise also the men, leaving the natural use of
the woman, burned in their lust for one another, men
with men committing what is shameful, and receiving
in themselves the penalty of their error which was
due.
28 And even as they did not like to retain God in their
knowledge, God gave them over to a debased mind, to
do those things which are not fitting;
29 being filled with all unrighteousness, sexual
immorality, wickedness, covetousness, maliciousness;
full of envy, murder, strife, deceit, evil-mindedness;
they are whisperers,
30 backbiters, haters of God, violent, proud, boasters,
inventors of evil things, disobedient to parents,
31 undiscerning, untrustworthy, unloving, unforgiv-
ing, unmerciful;
32 who, knowing the righteous judgment of God, that
those who practice such things are deserving of death,
not only do the same but also approve of those who
practice them.

These fifteen verses describe in some detail people who

have moved into darkness. God never intended for man to abide in darkness. Scripture clearly teaches that it is man's choice — not God's — that places him under the dominion of darkness. When men do this, they have exchanged the truth of God for a lie. They end up with debased or reprobate minds, minds which are without a standard of judgment.

I was born in 1936 and, even though I was raised in a home where we seldom went to church or read the Bible, I was taught a standard of judgment. My parents taught me right from wrong. Most people in our nation at that time were taught right from wrong. The standard of judgment that we were taught is called the Judeo-Christian ethic. We were taught the truths of right and wrong from God's Word, even though many of us didn't go to church or read the Bible!

For instance, I was taught that marriage was honorable, and that sex was for marriage. I was taught that pre-marital sex, adultery, homosexuality, and prostitution were wrong. I was taught that if a man did get a woman pregnant, the only right thing to do was to marry her.

Abortion was a word I never heard while growing up. In the 1930s, '40s, and '50s, we were given the light of God's Word, even though we were not Christians!

Today, the enemy, working as hard as he can, has succeeded in bringing **deep darkness** upon the unsaved people of our nation and the world!

Deep Darkness Upon the Nations

The Bible says, ". . .when the enemy comes in like a flood. . . . For behold, the darkness shall cover the earth, and deep darkness the people. . ." (Isa. 59:19b; 60:2a).

Today we are at the point that darkness is upon the earth and deep darkness the people. This is the very best effort of the enemy. The good news is that when the enemy comes in, God raises up His standard (Isa. 59:19b)!

God's Glory Upon the Church

ISAIAH 59:19-21
19 So shall they fear the name of the Lord from the west, and His glory from the rising of the sun; when the enemy comes in like a flood, the Spirit of the Lord will lift up a standard against him.
20 "The Redeemer will come to Zion, and to those who turn from transgression in Jacob," says the Lord.
21 "As for Me," says the Lord, "this is My covenant with them: My Spirit who is upon you, and My words which I have put in your mouth, shall not depart from your mouth, nor from the mouth of your descendants, nor from the mouth of your descendants' descendants," says the Lord, "from this time and forevermore."

ISAIAH 60:1-5
1 Arise, shine; for your light has come! And the GLORY of the Lord is risen UPON YOU.
2 For behold, the darkness shall cover the earth, and deep darkness the people; but the Lord will arise over you, and HIS GLORY will be seen UPON YOU.
3 The GENTILES shall COME to YOUR LIGHT, and kings to the brightness of your rising.
4 "Lift up your eyes all around, and see: they all gather together, they come to you; your sons shall

come from afar, and your daughters shall be nursed at
your side.
5   "Then you shall see and become radiant, and your
heart shall swell with joy; because the ABUNDANCE of
the SEA shall be TURNED to YOU, the wealth of the
GENTILES shall COME to YOU."

God's answer to the enemy bringing darkness upon
the earth, and deep darkness upon the people of the
nations, is so powerful that you need to read this passage of Scripture again — several times! First, His Spirit
that is upon us and His Word that He has put in our
mouths will not depart from us, our children, or our
grandchildren forever (Isa. 59:21)!

Then His glory will arise upon us, His Church, to
such an extent that it will be seen by all those in darkness. Then the nations will come to the light of His glory
upon us! The abundance of the sea — the nations — shall
come to us. This is the huge end-of-the-age harvest from
every nation, tribe, tongue and people coming to Jesus
through His Church. This harvest includes the Jews, for
it also includes those who turn from transgression in
Jacob.

So don't let this darkness, which you now see
upon the earth, depress you! God wants us to see
Him — who He is and what He is doing — more
than we see the enemy. We tend to forget that God
has a long history of working in the midst of enemy
opposition, and it has never deterred Him or moved
Him from His purposes for a moment. Even in Creation itself, He called light out of the midst of the
darkness.

Know that God is pouring out His glory upon His people. That glory will draw out of the darkness all who desire to know God.

Chapter VIII

JUDGMENT AND WRATH

There is a big difference between judgment and wrath. As I studied these words in W. E. Vines Expository Dictionary, the differences became obvious.

Judgment

Judgment is a decision that results from an investigation, where an act of distinguishing and separating takes place. This results in the rendering of a judgment. A judgment can be *for* you, resulting in a reward or blessing. Likewise, a judgment can be *against* you, resulting in a condemnation or curse.

One of the seven synonyms used for the Word of God, which are found in the first seven verses of Psalm 119, is **righteous judgments**. God's Word is called "righteous judgments."

Therefore, a person who is a doer of God's Word will be blessed in what he does (James 1:25).

Moses put it this way: "Then it shall come to pass, because you listen to these judgments, and keep and do them. . . . He will love you and bless you and multiply you; He will also bless. . . . You shall be blessed above all people. . ." (Deut. 7:12-14).

The other side of the coin is failure to be a doer of God's Word. A person may not obey God's Word because of a lack of knowledge of His Word, because of fear, rebellion, unbelief, or for many other reasons. However, whatever the reason for failing to obey and do God's Word, the result is the same. If you are not a consistent doer of the Word, you can't receive the rewards or blessings that flow to those who do the Word.

If a person not only fails to do what the Word tells us to do, but does what the Word warns us *not* to do, the result will be a judgment *against* — a curse. For instance, those who persist in sexual acts outside the marriage bed reap sickness, disease, mental anguish, destruction of relationships, or some other curse. These are judgments *against*. They are curses which result from doing things that God specifically tells us not to do.

God's Word is **law**. It is established and settled forever (Ps. 119:89). It will not change or go away. Heaven and earth may pass away, but God's Word will not pass away (Mark 13:31). God has set before us good and evil, blessing and cursing. We make the choices. The actions that follow our choices eventually result in judgments, either *for* us or *against* us. If we were just "half smart," we would always choose life and blessing! Let's not allow our flesh to rise up and cause us to make poor choices!

First Peter 4:17 says, "For the time has come for judgment to begin at the house of God; and if it begins with us first, what will be the end of those who do not obey the gospel of God?" We have seen the judgment of God increasing within His Church. God and His Word will continue to prune and weed, wash and cleanse, until He has a Body which will walk in His love, obey

His Word, and follow His Spirit. It will be through that body of believers that God will reap the huge harvest at the end of this age.

Wrath

W. E. Vine describes God's wrath in far more severe terms than judgment. He speaks of it in terms of an outburst of wrath from an inward indignation, which may issue in revenge. It quickly blazes up and then quickly subsides.

The two New Testament words translated anger — or fierceness — and wrath are used together only twice: in Revelation 16:19 ("the fierceness of His wrath") and Revelation 19:15 ("the fierceness and wrath of Almighty God").

God hears the voice of the blood of His children who were slain for the Word of God and for the testimony of Jesus. It has been crying to Him from the earth for several thousand years. It cries for justice and vengeance! The time will come when an outburst of wrath from God's inward indignation will quickly blaze up and issue forth in revenge for that blood! Justice and vengeance will come forth from God, upon the wicked, and upon the world system during God's "three woes."

Born-again ones won't have to receive any of God's wrath, because He already poured it out once, upon Jesus. Jesus took God's wrath for **my** sin and **yours** upon Himself! When we accepted Jesus and His sacrifice for us, He gave us His righteousness, His right-standing with God. Wow, what an exchange! We don't have to partake of God's wrath, because Jesus already took it for us!

ISAIAH 53:4-11

4   Surely He has borne our griefs and carried
our sorrows; yet we esteemed Him stricken, smit-
ten by God, and afflicted.

5   But He was wounded for our transgressions,
He was bruised for our iniquities; the chastise-
ment for our peace was upon Him, and by His
stripes we are healed.

6   All we like sheep have gone astray; we have
turned, every one, to his own way; and the Lord
has laid on Him the iniquity of us all.

7   He was oppressed and He was afflicted, yet He
opened not His mouth; He was led as a lamb to
the slaughter, and as a sheep before its shearers
is silent, so He opened not his mouth.

8   He was taken from prison and from judgment,
and who will declare His generation? For He was
cut off from the land of the living; for the transgressions of My people He was stricken.

9   And they made His grave with the wicked—but
with the rich at His death, because He had done
no violence, nor was any deceit in His mouth.

10 Yet it pleased the Lord to bruise Him; He has
put Him to grief. When You make His soul an
offering for sin, He shall see His seed, He shall
prolong His days, and the pleasure of the Lord
shall prosper in His hand.

11 He shall see the labor [travail] of His soul, and
be satisfied. By His knowledge My righteous Servant shall justify many, for He shall bear their
iniquities.

For centuries, Satan has deceived the nations
concerning both judgment and wrath. Some
churches have even taught that God was viewing

man from His throne with an intent to punish.

In fact, nothing could be further from the truth! No born-again believer will have to suffer the wrath of God. Jesus has done it for us: "and to wait for His Son from heaven, whom He raised from the dead, even Jesus who **delivers us from the wrath** to come. . . . For God did not appoint us to wrath, but to obtain salvation through our Lord Jesus Christ" (I Thess. 1:10; 5:9).

Chapter IX

SALVATION FOR THE JEWS

It would be helpful for you to read Ezekiel chapters 36 through 39 before you proceed in this book. Read all four chapters straight through. These four chapters tell the story of the salvation of the Jews.

This story starts with God speaking to the land of Israel which had become ". . .desolate wastes. . .and mockery to the rest of the nations all around" (Ezek. 36:4). God speaks to the land and says, "But you, O mountains of Israel, you shall shoot forth your branches and yield your fruit to My people Israel, for they are about to come. For indeed I am for you, and I will turn to you, and you shall be tilled and sown. I will multiply men upon you, **all** the **house** of **Israel**, all of it; and the cities shall be inhabited and the ruins rebuilt" (vv. 8-10).

During my lifetime, I have had the privilege of seeing the land of Israel transformed from a desolate wasteland to a fertile, productive land. I've been thrilled to watch God as He is bringing the **whole house** of Israel back to their land. Some are yet to come, but they have been coming rapidly from throughout the whole earth — from wherever He has scattered them! Why?

EZEKIEL 36:19-23

19 "So I scattered them among the nations, and they were **dispersed throughout the countries; I judged them**

according to their ways and their deeds.
20 "When they came to the nations, wherever they went, they PROFANED MY HOLY NAME—when they said of them, 'These are the people of the Lord, and yet they have gone out of His land.'
21 "But I had concern for MY HOLY NAME, which the house of Israel had profaned among the nations wherever they went.
22 "Therefore say to the house of Israel, 'Thus says the Lord God: "I do not do this for your sake, O house of Israel, BUT FOR MY HOLY NAME'S sake, which you have profaned among the nations wherever you went.
23 "And I WILL SANCTIFY MY GREAT NAME, which has been profaned among the nations, which you have profaned in their midst; and the NATIONS SHALL KNOW that I AM THE LORD," says the Lord God, "when I am hallowed in you before their eyes."'"

God scattered the Jews among the nations as judgment for their deeds and their ways. During all this time of their exile into the nations, they have profaned His holy Name. They said they were the people of the Lord, but they have profaned His holy Name. Now God is restoring them to their land, not for their sakes, but for the **sake** of **His holy Name**, and so the **nations may know Him!**

His Holy Name

PHILIPPIANS 2:5-11
5   Let this mind be in you which was also in Christ Jesus,
6   who, being in the form of God, did not consider it robbery to be equal with God,
7   but made Himself of no reputation, taking the form of a bondservant, and coming in the likeness of men.

8   And being found in appearance as a man, He hum-
bled Himself and became obedient to the point of death,
even the death of the cross.
9   Therefore God also has highly exalted Him and given
Him THE NAME which is ABOVE EVERY NAME,
10 that at the NAME OF JESUS every knee should bow,
of those in heaven, and of those on earth, and of those
under the earth,
11 and that every tongue should confess that JESUS
CHRIST IS LORD, to the glory of God the Father.

The Name of the Lord, His holy Name, is **Jesus
Christ**! It was bestowed upon Him by the Father because
of His obedience — even to His death on the Cross — to
complete the Father's plan for the redemption of mankind.

Since the time the Jews completed their final disperse-
ment into the nations, about 70 AD, they have continued
to profane the Holy Name of Jesus Christ. They have
claimed to be God's people, but they have rejected their
Savior.

Restoration

EZEKIEL 37:10-14
10 So I prophesied as He commanded me, and breath
came into them, and they lived, and stood upon their
feet, an exceedingly great army.
11 Then He said to me, "Son of man, these bones are the
WHOLE HOUSE of ISRAEL. They indeed say, 'Our bones
are dry, our hope is lost, and we ourselves are cut off!'
12 "Therefore prophesy and say to them, 'Thus says the
Lord God: "Behold, O My people, I will open your graves
and cause you to come up from your graves, and bring
you into the land of Israel.

13 "Then you shall know that I am the Lord, when I have opened your graves, O My people, and brought you up from your graves.
14 "I will put My Spirit in you, and you shall live, and I will place you in your own land. Then you shall know that I, the Lord, have spoken it and performed it," says the Lord.'"

God is restoring the Jews to their land, connecting "bone to bone," and they are getting flesh put upon their bones and becoming a nation of the whole house of Israel.

EZEKIEL 36:25-27
25 "Then I will sprinkle clean water on you, and you shall be clean; I will cleanse you from all your filthiness and from all your idols.
26 "I will give you a new heart and put a new spirit within you; I will take the heart of stone out of your flesh and give you a heart of flesh.
27 "I will put My Spirit within you and cause you to walk in My statutes, and you will keep My judgments and do them."

God will put His spirit in them. They will be born again, just like you and I are born again. There are many "completed" or born-again Jews today. However, as a nation, they are still the lost sheep of the house of Israel. When a Jew today receives Jesus into his heart, he is rejected by his Jewish family and friends. The majority of Jews still profane His holy Name. But God will change this. He will open the eyes of the **Jews and the nations** as to who Jesus is!

How?

EZEKIEL 38:1-4,8,16,18-23

1   Now the word of the Lord came to me, saying,

2   "Son of man, set your face against Gog, of the land of Magog, the prince of Rosh, Meshech, and Tubal, and prophesy against him,

3   "and say, 'Thus says the Lord God: "Behold, I am against you, O Gog, the prince of Rosh, Meshech, and Tubal.

4   "I will turn you around, put hooks in your jaws, and lead you out, with all your army, horses, and horsemen, all splendidly clothed, a great company with bucklers and shields, all of them handling swords. . . .

8   "After many days you will be visited. In the latter years you will come into the land of those brought back from the sword and gathered from many people on the mountains of Israel, which had long been desolate; they were brought out of the nations, and now all of them dwell safely. . . .'"

16   "You will come up against My people Israel like a cloud, to cover the land. It will be in the latter days that I WILL BRING YOU AGAINST MY LAND, SO THAT THE NATIONS MAY KNOW ME, when I am hallowed in you, O Gog, before their eyes. . . ."

18   "And it will come to pass at the same time, when Gog comes against the land of Israel," says the Lord God, "that My fury will show in My face.

19   "For in My jealousy and in the fire of My wrath I have spoken: 'Surely in that day there shall be a great earthquake in the land of Israel,

20   'so that the fish of the sea, the birds of the heavens, the beasts of the fields, all creeping things that creep on the earth, and ALL MEN who are ON the FACE of the EARTH shall SHAKE at MY PRESENCE. The mountains shall be thrown down, the steep places shall fall, and every wall shall fall to the ground.'

21 "I will call for a sword against Gog throughout all My mountains," says the Lord God. "Every man's sword will be against his brother.

22 "And I will bring him to judgment with pestilence and bloodshed; I will rain down on him, on his troops, and on the many peoples who are with him, flooding rain, great hailstones, fire, and brimstone.

23 "Thus I will magnify Myself and sanctify Myself, and I WILL BE KNOWN in the EYES of MANY NATIONS. Then THEY SHALL KNOW that I am the Lord.'"

EZEKIEL 39:6,7

6 "And I will send fire on Magog and on those who live in security in the coastlands. Then they shall know that I am the Lord.

7 "So I will MAKE MY HOLY NAME KNOWN in the MIDST of MY PEOPLE ISRAEL, and I will NOT let them PROFANE MY HOLY NAME ANYMORE. Then the NATIONS shall KNOW that I am the Lord, the Holy One in Israel."

A time is coming when the nation of Israel will feel safe and at peace. This process of bringing peace between Israel and its neighbors has been going on for several years. It is a slow, hard process, but it will be completed. Then, when Israel believes it is finally safe and at peace, God will bring a large army down upon the land of Israel. Then God will bring forth the greatest earthquake in the history of mankind to this time. He will bring this large army to judgment in the land of Israel.

This judgment of God will be so severe, it will require seven months for the Jews to bury the remains of the army which have not been eaten by the birds and the beasts. It will take seven years for the Jews to dispose of the weapons left in their land.

This great earthquake and severe judgment of God is **performed by God** to **make His holy Name known** in the **midst** of **His people Israel, and,** so that the **nations might know** Him! This great and powerful event, done by the mighty hand of God, will open the eyes of the Jews, and the nations to **Jesus Christ**! It will be the final event that opens the nations to the final great harvest at the end of this age — the final response to the blood of Jesus!

After this event, the Jews will come into the Kingdom, and the trumpets of harvest will blow!

Chapter X

THE WHOLE HOUSE OF ISRAEL

Throughout the story in Ezekiel chapters 36 through 39, God makes it clear that He is going to restore the whole house of Israel to their land and then reveal His holy Name (Jesus Christ) to them. Please understand that not every Jew will return to Israel, nor will every Jew receive Jesus. God is saying here that He will bring a remnant, a people descended from each of the Twelve Tribes, back to the land of Israel. Then a remnant from each of these tribes will be saved.

It's important for us to realize that the Jews were brought back to their land once before, from Babylon. However, that restoration did not include the whole house of Israel. God makes it absolutely clear that He will bring back the **whole house** of Israel and reveal His holy Name to them for their salvation. The events that open their eyes to the truth are a tremendous earthquake and judgment, by God, on the army of Gog.

Let me show you this picture in The Revelation of Jesus Christ. Compare this passage of Scripture with Ezekiel 38:19,20.

REVELATION 6:12-17
12 I looked when He opened the sixth seal, and behold, there was a great earthquake; and the sun

53

became black as sackcloth of hair, and the moon
became like blood.
13 And the stars of heaven fell to the earth, as a fig
tree drops its late figs when it is shaken by a mighty
wind.
14 Then the sky receded as a scroll when it is rolled
up, and every mountain and island was moved out of
its place.
15 And the kings of the earth, the great men, the rich
men, the commanders, the mighty men, every slave
and every free man, hid themselves in the caves and in
the rocks of the mountains,
16 and said to the mountains and rocks, "Fall on us
and hide us from the face of Him who sits on the
throne and from the wrath of the Lamb!
17 "For the great day of His wrath has come, and who
is able to stand?"

The men of the nations now recognize that there is a
God in Heaven and a Lamb in Heaven! These men, however, mistake this severe judgment of God for His
wrath! But, no, this isn't His wrath. He has brought this
severe judgment so that the nations may know Him and
so that the Jews will know His holy Name, Jesus
Christ! Now watch what happens!

REVELATION 7:1-4
1   After these things I saw four angels standing at the
four corners of the earth. . . .
2   Then I saw another angel ascending from the east,
having the seal of the living God. And he cried with a
loud voice to the four angels to whom it was granted
to harm the earth and the sea,
3   saying, "Do not harm the earth, the sea, or the trees

till we have sealed the servants of our God on their foreheads."
4   And I heard the number of those who were sealed. One hundred and forty-four thousand of ALL the TRIBES of the children of ISRAEL were sealed.

The next event after this great earthquake, in which all the men of the earth realize that there is a God in Heaven, is that a remnant of **all** the **tribes** of Israel, the **whole house** of Israel, will get sealed. They will get sealed the same way that you and I got sealed: by the Holy Spirit of promise.

The forehead symbolizes our choice — our will. They choose Jesus as Lord and Savior, and they get sealed. God is no respecter of persons. We all come to Him the same way, through the blood of Jesus.

God will have just opened the eyes of the nations and the Jews to the reality of Jesus Christ! Some will hate Him and blaspheme Him, but they surely will know that there is a God in Heaven!

Chapter XI

THE MYSTERY OF GOD

*. . .in the days of the sounding of the **seventh angel**, when he is **about** to sound, the **mystery of God** would be **finished**, as He declared to His servants the prophets.*

— Revelation 10:7

I now rejoice in my sufferings for you, and fill up in my flesh what is lacking in the afflictions of Christ, for the sake of His body, which is the church,

*of which I became a minister according to the stewardship from God which was given to me for you, to **fulfill** the **word** of **God**,*

*the **mystery** which has been hidden from ages and from generations, but now has been revealed to His saints.*

*To them God willed to make known what are the riches of the glory of this **mystery** among the Gentiles: which **is Christ in you**, the **hope of glory**.*

— Colossians 1:24-27

The explanation of this mystery was given by God to Paul to fulfill the Word of God. This mystery had been hidden in ages past, but God chose to reveal it to His Church through the Apostle Paul. This mystery was not taught or understood until after the resurrection of Jesus Christ.

This mystery is Christ in us (you and me), the hope of glory. What we hope for, we **do not yet have** (Rom. 8:24)! We do have Christ in us through the indwelling presence of the Holy Spirit. And we do have a measure of the glory of God that can and does manifest upon us. But we do not yet have this mystery, for we still hope for it.

What we have today is the *earnest* or the *down-payment* or *first installment* for this hope of glory. We have the indwelling presence of the Holy Spirit who has re-created our inward man, our spirit man. We have a brand-new, eternal man on the inside that is infused by God Himself.

That is our down-payment, our earnest, the first-fruits for that final hope, which is a **glorified body**!

Today, our outward man, our body, is not eternal. Our outward man is mortal and subject to decay and death. However, the Lord Jesus Christ is seated in Heaven, waiting.

PSALM 110:1
1   The Lord said to my lord, "Sit at My right hand, till I make Your enemies Your footstool."

HEBREWS 10:12,13
12 But this Man, after He had offered one sacrifice for sins forever, sat down at the right hand of God,
13 from that time waiting till His enemies are made His footstool.

I CORINTHIANS 15:26
26 The LAST ENEMY that will be destroyed is DEATH.

All of us whose inward man has passed from spiritual death to spiritual life will one day go from having a mortal body to having an immortal body. We will have a **body** which is glorified — a body saturated with the presence and power of God — a body that will never die! The last enemy of God's children, physical death, will have been placed under the feet of Jesus.

Today, the only glorified body in the Church belongs to the Head of the Church, Jesus Christ. Jesus is the only One who has been resurrected into a glorified body. Many people have been resuscitated to life. However, no one but Jesus has ever died physically, been resurrected with a glorified body, and then caught up to Heaven. Flesh and blood cannot inherit the Kingdom of God. But all of us who have Christ in us have this hope!

This great mystery was revealed by God to the Apostle Paul. Paul taught it to the churches.

I CORINTHIANS 15:20-26,35-38,44,49-54
**20 But now Christ is risen from the dead, and has become the firstfruits of those who have fallen asleep.
21 For since by man came death, by Man also came the resurrection of the dead.
22 For as in Adam all die, even so in Christ all SHALL be made alive.
23 But each one in his own order: Christ the first-fruits, afterward those who are Christ's AT HIS COMING.
24 Then comes the end, when He delivers the kingdom to God the Father, when He puts an end to all rule and all authority and power.
25 For He must reign till He has put all enemies under His feet.**

26 The LAST ENEMY that will be destroyed is DEATH....
35 But someone will say, "How are the dead raised up? And with what body do they come?"
36 Foolish one, what you sow is not made alive unless it dies.
37 And what you sow, you do not sow that body that SHALL be, but mere grain—perhaps wheat or some other grain.
38 But God gives it a body as He pleases, and to each seed its own body....
44 It is sown a natural body, it is raised a spiritual body....
49 And as we have borne the image of the man of dust, we SHALL also bear the image of the heavenly Man.
50 Now this I say, brethren, that flesh and blood cannot inherit the kingdom of God; nor does corruption inherit incorruption.
51 Behold, I tell you a MYSTERY: We shall not all sleep, but WE SHALL ALL BE CHANGED—
52 in a moment, in the twinkling of an eye, at the LAST TRUMPET. For the trumpet will sound, and the dead will be raised incorruptible, and we shall be changed.
53 For this corruptible must put on incorruption, and this mortal must put on immortality.
54 So when this corruptible has put on incorruption, and this mortal has put on immortality, then shall be brought to pass the saying that is written: "Death is swallowed up in victory."

The following is how Paul taught this mystery to the Church at Rome.

ROMANS 8:10,11,18-25
10 And if Christ is in you, the body is dead because of sin, but the Spirit is life because of righteousness.

11 But if the Spirit of Him who raised Jesus from the dead dwells in you, He who raised Christ from the dead WILL also give life to your mortal bodies through His Spirit who dwells in you. . . .
18 For I consider that the sufferings of this present time are not worthy to be compared with the GLORY which SHALL be revealed in us.
19 For the earnest expectation of the creation EAGERLY WAITS for the revealing of the sons of God.
20 For the creation was subjected to futility, not willingly, but because of Him who subjected it in HOPE;
21 BECAUSE the CREATION itself ALSO WILL BE delivered from the bondage of corruption into the glorious liberty of the children of God.
22 For we know that the WHOLE CREATION GROANS and labors with birth pangs together until now.
23 Not only that, but we also who have the firstfruits of the Spirit, even we ourselves GROAN within ourselves, eagerly WAITING FOR the adoption, THE REDEMPTION OF OUR BODY.
24 For we were saved in this HOPE, but hope that is seen is not hope; for why does one still hope for what he sees?
25 But if we hope for what we do not see, we eagerly wait for it with perseverance.

I don't know about you, but I am eagerly awaiting the redemption of my body! It is spiritually dead now, because of sin, so it cannot inherit the Kingdom of God. There is a nature of sin in my body so that this body of flesh lusts against my spirit, and my spirit against my flesh.

Until my body is changed, it cannot stand in the presence of God in Heaven! But my body shall be made alive by the indwelling Holy Spirit! I have that promise and that great hope!

In fact, the whole creation is in bondage. The creation itself is waiting to be freed from bondage and moved into the glorious liberty of the children of God!

The truth is, we are half-alive children right now. Our inward man is alive to God, but because of the nature of sin in our flesh, our bodies can't go to Heaven and stand in the presence of God. In fact, our bodies have a difficult time surviving a strong manifestation of the glory of God upon them and through them. Our bodies have difficulty surviving extended periods of the fire or glory of God. But all of that will change in the days of the sounding of the seventh angel.

Because when he is **about** to sound, the **mystery** of **God** will be **finished!**

Chapter XII

THE WHEAT AND THE TARES

Another parable He [Jesus] put forth to them, saying: "The kingdom of heaven is like a man who sowed good seed in his field;

"but while men slept, his enemy came and sowed tares among the wheat and went his way.

"But when the grain had sprouted and produced a crop, then the tares also appeared.

"So the servants of the owner came and said to him, 'Sir, did you not sow good seed in your field? How then does it have tares?'

"He said to them, 'An enemy has done this.' The servants said to him, 'Do you want us then to go and gather them up?'

"But he said, 'No, lest while you gather up the tares you also uproot the wheat with them.

'Let both grow together until the harvest, and at the time of harvest I will say to the reapers, "First gather together the tares and bind them in bundles to burn them, but gather the wheat into my barn."'"

— Matthew 13:24-30

The following verses explain "the parable of the tares of the field."

MATTHEW 13:36-43

36 Then Jesus sent the multitude away and went into the house. And His disciples came to Him, saying, "Explain to us the parable of the tares of the field."

37 He answered and said to them: "He who sows the good seed is the Son of Man.

38 "The FIELD is the WORLD, the good seeds are the sons of the kingdom, but the TARES are the SONS of the WICKED ONE.

39 "The enemy who sowed them is the devil, the HARVEST is the END of THE AGE, and the REAPERS are the ANGELS.

40 "Therefore as the tares are gathered and burned in the fire, so it will be at the end of this age.

41 "The Son of Man will send out His angels, and they will gather out of His kingdom all things that offend, and those who practice lawlessness,

42 "and will cast them into the furnace of fire. There will be wailing and gnashing of teeth.

43 "Then the RIGHTEOUS will SHINE FORTH AS the SUN IN the KINGDOM of THEIR FATHER. He who has ears to hear, let him hear!"

These scriptures refer specifically to the harvest at the end of this age — the harvest that is swiftly approaching! To successfully reap this huge harvest from the whole earth, the tares must first be removed from the harvest field.

Servants harvest wheat, but **angels reap** the **tares!** You and I cannot see the hearts of men. We don't know if they are serving the devil or if they are just lost souls. We fellow servants would do more harm than good if we tried to remove the tares! So in this great, supernatural harvest at the end of this age, God will send His angels to remove the tares.

Let's look at what happens during the great earthquake of the sixth seal as God opens the eyes of the Jews and the nations to the reality of Jesus Christ.

"I looked when He opened the sixth seal, and behold, there was a great earthquake; and the sun became black as sackcloth of hair, and the moon became like blood. And the **stars** of **heaven** fell to the earth, as a fig tree drops its late figs when it is shaken by a mighty wind" (Rev. 6:12,13).

Stars are symbolic of angels, God's angels of Heaven. Late figs are very ripe and full. When the tree is shaken by a mighty wind, they all come crashing to the ground. When the mighty wind of the Holy Spirit blows, the angels of God will come swiftly to the earth, and we will experience a ministry of angels in behalf of Jesus' fellow servants — the likes of which have never before been seen! The angels will remove the tares, sometimes by the thousands at a time, so the harvest field can be reached!

As the tares are removed, the glory of God will shine forth as the sun upon the righteous in His kingdom. Remember, God will take care of the tares by His reapers, the angels. Our job is to follow the leadership of the Holy Spirit in preaching, teaching, and demonstrating His Word, His love, and His power. Then the wheat will be brought into His barn!

Chapter XIII

THE DAYS BEFORE
THE SEVENTH TRUMPET

Two Witnesses

"And I will give power to my two witnesses, and they will prophesy one thousand two hundred and sixty days, clothed in sackcloth."

These are the two olive trees and the two lampstands standing before the God of the earth.

And if anyone wants to harm them, fire proceeds from their mouth and devours their enemies. And if anyone wants to harm them, he must be killed in this manner.

These have power to shut heaven, so that no rain falls in the days of their prophecy; and they have power over waters to turn them to blood, and to strike the earth with all plagues, as often as they desire.

When they finish their testimony, the beast that ascends out of the bottomless pit will make war against them, overcome them, and kill them.

And their dead bodies will lie in the street of the great city which spiritually is called Sodom and Egypt, where also our Lord was crucified.

Then those from the peoples, tribes, tongues, and nations will see their dead bodies three-and-a-half days, and not allow their dead bodies to be put into graves.

And those who dwell on the earth will rejoice over them, make merry, and send gifts to one another, because these two prophets tormented those who dwell on the earth.

*Now after the three-and-a-half days the **breath of life** from God entered them, and they stood on their feet, and great fear fell on those who saw them.*

*And they heard a loud **voice** from **heaven** saying to them, "**Come up here.**" And they ascended to heaven in a cloud, and their enemies saw them. . . .*

Then the seventh angel sounded: And there were loud voices in heaven, saying, "The kingdoms of this world have become the kingdoms of our Lord and of His Christ, and He shall reign forever and ever!"

— Revelation 11:3-12,15

In the days before the sounding of the seventh angel, we see two prophets of God who minister for three and a half years. They walk in the same anointing as Jesus did during His three and a half years of ministry upon the earth. No one could harm Jesus, and no one can harm *them*, until their ministry is **finished**.

When their ministry is finished, they are killed. The Body of Christ — those from the peoples, tribes, tongues, and nations whose citizenship is in Heaven — will not allow their bodies to be buried!

Jesus said, "...After three days I will rise" (Matt. 27:63). Sure enough, after three days, He was resurrected. And in three and a half days, the breath of life from God entered the two witnesses, and they stood on their feet. A voice from Heaven said, "**Come up here!**" (Rev. 11:12).

I THESSALONIANS 4:16,17
16 For the Lord Himself will descend from heaven

with a SHOUT, with the voice of an archangel, and with the trumpet of God. And the dead in Christ will rise first.

17 Then we who are alive and remain shall be caught up TOGETHER with them in the clouds to meet the Lord in the air. And thus we shall always be with the Lord.

Prior to this final harvest of trumpets, God always had **a prophet**. From the time of Abraham to Jesus, it was **a Jew**. From shortly after the time of Jesus until the present time, it has been primarily **a Gentile**. However, during these final trumpets of harvest, God has **two** prophets. He has the Jew and the Gentile together in Christ! I believe that during this three and a half years of final harvest, there may be two major prophets of God. But, **symbolically**, I believe they represent the Jew and the Gentile together in Christ — a **completed Body of Christ** — walking this earth and proclaiming the Gospel of the Kingdom for three and a half years just like Jesus walked the earth (Israel) during His three and a half years of ministry.

I believe this Body will walk in the full corporate anointing of the Lord. We will have the complete ministry and manifestation of angels to assist us, and the power and demonstration of the Holy Spirit to do the works of Jesus!

At the close of this final ministry of His Body in the earth, when the Gospel has been preached to every creature, the Father will turn to Jesus and say, "Go, bring My family home."

The dead in Christ will rise in glorified bodies, and you and I who remain will have our bodies changed. The last enemy of His children, **physical death**, will be put under the feet of Jesus. We will all go up **together**, to meet Him in the air!

Chapter XIV

JUDGMENT, WRATH,
AND REWARD

*Then the **seventh angel sounded**: And there were loud voices in heaven, saying, "The kingdoms of this world have become the kingdoms of our Lord and of His Christ, and He shall reign forever and ever!"*

And the twenty-four elders who sat before God on their thrones fell on their faces and worshiped God,

saying: "We give You thanks, O Lord God Almighty, the One who is and who was and who is to come, because You have taken Your great power and reigned.

*"The nations were angry, and Your **wrath** has come, and the time of the dead, that they should be **judged**, and that You should **reward** Your servants the prophets and the saints, and those who fear Your name, small and great, and should destroy those who destroy the earth."*

— Revelation 11:15-18

When the seventh angel sounds, the time will have arrived for the three actions by God: *judgment, wrath,* and *reward.*

Judgment and Wrath

"The nations were angry, and Your wrath has come, and

the time of the dead, that they should be judged. . .and should destroy those who destroy the earth" (Rev. 11:18).

Remember back in the history of the Church when the fifth seal was opened. John saw under the altar of God in Heaven the souls of those who had been slain for the Word of God and for the testimony of Jesus.

They cried out to God, asking how long it would be until He would judge and avenge their blood on those who dwell on the earth. God's answer to them was to wait a little longer, until both the number of their brethren and fellow servants who would be killed was completed.

Now in Revelation chapter 11, the killing of God's servants has been completed. The two witnesses who were killed in Jerusalem after they **finished** their testimony were the last witnesses. God has just brought His family home, and now is the time to **judge** the **dead**. The dead which God now judges are the **spiritually** dead who remain upon the earth.

Remember, the twenty-four elders have just announced that the nations were angry and that God's wrath and the time of the judgment of the dead has come. God will pour out His wrath to judge and avenge the blood of the righteous. The spiritually dead — the wicked, the blasphemers, and the haters and mockers of God — will receive His judgments and taste His wrath. God will bring down, once and for all, Mystery Babylon the Great, mother of harlots and of the abominations of the earth.

Reward

". . .And that You should **reward Your servants** the prophets and the saints, and those who fear Your name, small and great. . ." (Rev. 11:18).

At the same time that God's final judgment and wrath are being poured out upon those who are spiritually dead and who destroy the earth, God's family has been taken to Heaven. It is our time to receive **eternal rewards!**

Judgment Seat of Christ

Paul, writing to the Corinthians admonishes them to ". . .make it our aim, whether present or absent, to be well pleasing to Him. For we must all appear before the judgment seat of Christ, that each one may receive the things done in the body, according to what he has done, whether good or bad" (II Cor. 5:9,10).

I CORINTHIANS 3:11-15
11 For no other foundation can anyone lay than that which is laid, which is Jesus Christ.
12 Now if anyone builds on this foundation with gold, silver, precious stones, wood, hay, straw,
13 each one's work will become clear; for the Day will declare it, because it will be revealed by fire; and the fire will test each one's work, of what sort it is.
14 If anyone's work which he has built on it endures, he will receive a REWARD.
15 If anyone's work is burned, he will SUFFER LOSS; but he himself will be saved, yet so as through fire.

"Let us be glad and rejoice and give Him glory, for the marriage of the Lamb has come, and His wife has made herself ready. And to her it was granted to be arrayed in **fine linen**, clean and bright, for the fine linen is the **righteous acts** of the saints. Then he said to me, 'Write: "Blessed are those who are called to the marriage supper of the Lamb!"'" (Rev. 19:7-9).

Reward or Loss?

As we study these scriptures, they reveal some very sobering truths. First, when you and I stand before God, the works which we have done here in the flesh since we received Jesus will be judged by Him. If these works were in obedience to His Word and His will, under the direction of His Spirit, and for His glory (reflective in the Scriptures of gold, silver and precious stones), we will receive a **reward**.

If, on the other hand, after receiving Jesus, we still followed our own word and will, according to the appetites of our flesh and for our promotion (reflective of wood, hay and straw), we will **suffer loss**. We are saved but will suffer loss.

Then as we look at the Marriage Supper of Jesus, we see the bride clothed in **fine linen**, which are the **righteous acts** of the saints. The word used here for fine linen is different from the word used for white robe. As you study, you'll see we all get a white robe when we get to Heaven. However, only those saints who have done righteous acts have a **fine linen** wedding garment.

Blessed are those who are called to the Marriage Supper of the Lamb! We determine how far we go with Jesus by the **choices** we make and our **actions** that follow!

Another very sobering scripture relating to this is found in Second Corinthians 5, where Paul is teaching about the inward man and the outward man. He talks about how our inward man is groaning, earnestly desiring to have a body, an outward man, that also is from God above.

"For in this we groan, earnestly desiring to be clothed with our habitation which is from heaven, if indeed, having been clothed, we shall not be found **naked**" (II Cor. 5:2,3).

It is a very sobering thought that some Christians could receive their glorified bodies, yet having done so, end up being naked. I don't know about you, but I expect to receive fine linen and to be invited to the Marriage Supper. If you're not serving God with your whole heart, now would be a good time to make the necessary adjustments in your life. The time is short!

Chapter XV

A BAPTISM OF FIRE

*I [John the Baptist] indeed baptize you with water unto repentance, but He who is coming after me is mightier than I, whose sandals I am not worthy to carry. He will baptize you **with** the Holy Spirit and fire.*

*His winnowing fan is in His hand, and He will thoroughly clean out His threshing floor, and gather His wheat into the barn; but He will **burn up** the **chaff** with unquenchable fire.*

— Matthew 3:11,12

Today the fire of God is falling upon the hungry hearts of His children throughout the earth. On every continent and in every land, those whose hearts are hungering and thirsting for Jesus are experiencing the cleansing power of Holy Spirit fire in their hearts.

Most of us in the Body of Christ have "chaff" in our hearts. Just listen to what comes out of our mouths and you can readily see that we have problems with pride, selfishness, judgmentalism, anger, hurt, envy, lust, fear, unforgiveness, and other forms of "chaff." These are attitudes and motives of our heart which must go. Some of us have been trying for years to change and to rid ourselves of these destructive attitudes and motives. For the most part, we've met with marginal success.

God, on the other hand, needs a people whose hearts are pure. He needs a people whose hearts are filled with His love, His joy, and His presence. He needs a people whose **hearts** are **without spot** or **wrinkle**.

"Husbands, love your wives, just as Christ also loved the church and gave Himself for her, that He might sanctify and cleanse her with the washing of water by the word, that He might present her to Himself a glorious church, **not having spot** or **wrinkle** or **any such thing**, but that she should **be holy** and **without blemish**" (Eph. 5:25-27).

I thank God for many years of washing by His Word! However, after seventeen years of great Word teaching and preaching, I found my heart still had a few spots and wrinkles. It was not totally pure and without blemish.

Three years ago, as my heart was crying out to Jesus to be more like Him, I came under the fire of the Holy Spirit. The anointing was so strong that I was "glued" to the floor and couldn't move for over thirty minutes. God talked to my heart during that time and told me I could go no further in His plan for my life until I got rid of judgmentalism in my heart. I had been making mental judgments about people, about brothers and sisters in the Lord. I couldn't see their hearts, yet I was making mental judgments about them. Sometimes I would even give voice to those judgments.

I thought about what the Lord told me during that encounter but didn't completely repent.

Four months later, at another meeting where the cleansing fire of the Holy Spirit was falling, I cried out to God to please take every ounce of judgmentalism out of my heart. I never wanted to have another judgmental thought or speak another word of judgment concerning a member of God's family.

Almost instantly, God's fire fell upon me and completely cleansed my heart of all judgmentalism. He replaced it with more of His love, His joy, and His peace. My conscience is now very tender in that area. At the first sign of a judgmental thought, it fires off a warning, and I **cast** the **thought down**. The word God gave me was, **"Take no thought."**

God Looks on Our Heart

"But the Lord said to Samuel, 'Do not look at his appearance or at his physical stature, because I have refused him. For the Lord does not see as man sees; for man looks at the outward appearance, but the **Lord looks at** the **heart**'" (I Sam. 16:7).

It is important for us to understand that God looks on our heart. The **attitudes** and the **motives** of our **heart must be pure** if we desire to be a fellow servant of the Lord — to be used by Him during this huge, end-of-this-age harvest. Some of us have wrong attitudes and wrong motives in our heart that we do not recognize. Others of us have wrong attitudes and wrong motives that we don't want to admit or don't want to let go of. All of this "chaff" must be cleansed from our hearts before God will put His glory, His anointing, upon us. **We must go through His fire if we are to fulfill His purpose in our lives.**

During the past several years, God's cleansing fire has been falling in great measure upon the hungry hearts in His Church throughout the earth. It is intensifying and spreading as more and more of His **people** become **hungry to be like Jesus**. We must desire to be free from the hidden sins of our heart and to be holy, filled only with Jesus and His love. As we hunger and thirst for Jesus, the **cleansing fire** of God will **remove** the **spots** and the **wrinkles** from our **hearts**. Then He will fill us with His love, His joy, His peace, and His presence. It is truly a joy **unspeakable** and **full** of **glory**!

A Pure and Obedient Army

God is raising up the army which He will use for the final harvest of the earth. It does not have to be a large army because God will move with the greatest display of supernatural signs, wonders, miracles, and judgments ever seen or experienced by mankind. No, it doesn't need to be a large army, but it **must be** a **pure** and **obedient** army!

JUDGES 7:2-4,7
2   And the Lord said to Gideon, "The people who are with you are too many for Me to give the Midianites into their hands, lest Israel claim glory for itself against Me, saying, 'My own hand has saved me.'
3   "Now therefore, proclaim in the hearing of the people, saying, 'Whoever is fearful and afraid, let him turn and depart at once from Mount Gilead.'" And twenty-two thousand of the people returned, and ten thousand remained.

4   But the Lord said to Gideon, "The people are still too many; bring them down to the water, and I WILL TEST THEM for you there. Then it will be, that of whom I say to you, 'This one shall go with you,' the same shall go with you. ..."
7   Then the Lord said to Gideon, "By the three hundred men who lapped I will save you, and deliver the Midianites into your hand. Let all the other people go, every man to his place."

Just as God tested the army of Gideon, so will He test the attitudes and motives of our hearts. We **must** have a **pure heart**, without spot or wrinkle, to qualify for the manifestation of God's glory upon us and flowing through us. It is with that glory, that anointing or power of God, that He will harvest the entire earth. Each vessel that holds His glory must be pure. We **must go through His cleansing fire**! We need to get under the fire, get in the fire, and **stay** in the fire.

Then He will cleanse our hearts and **keep** them **pure**. We will remain immersed in our first love, who is Jesus, as long as we stay close to His fire.

How do we get in the fire? By having a heart that is hungry, hungry, hungry for Jesus! By having a heart that is so hungry that we don't put anything ahead of Jesus. By having a hunger to be conformed to His image. By having a hunger to be like Jesus and to have the love and joy and compassion of Jesus fill us to overflowing.

Have a desire for a **pure** and **holy** heart. Let the **Word** of God be your **guide** and the **fire** of the Holy Spirit your **purifying flame**.

Chapter XVI

GOD'S RAIN

The Latter Rain

But Peter, standing up with the eleven, raised his voice and said to them, "Men of Judea and all who dwell in Jerusalem, let this be known to you, and heed my words.

"For these are not drunk, as you suppose, since it is only the third hour of the day.

*"But this is what was spoken by the prophet Joel: 'And it shall come to pass in the **last** days, says God, that I will pour out of My Spirit on all flesh. . . .'"*

— Acts 2:14-16

Peter went on to tell the people about some of the manifestations of God's Spirit that would take place in this **latter** rain of the **last** days. He finished this list of manifestations with, "And it shall come to pass that **whoever calls** on the **name** of the **Lord** shall be **saved**" (Acts 2:21).

The latter rain of God's power arrived with the ministry of Jesus. He was anointed by the Holy Spirit and power to do good and to destroy the works of the devil (Acts 10:38). On the day of Pentecost, that anointing or power of the Holy Spirit was poured out upon the Church.

This **latter** rain is **characterized** by the **love, mercy,** and **grace** of God, **leading people to** repentance

and **salvation** through Jesus. It covers the Age of
Grace, from Jesus' first coming until His second coming
to this earth. It can be looked at as: **early rain** from the
time of Jesus through the third-century Church; **middle rain**, the church in Reformation; and **late rain**, the
huge outpouring of God's power through the Holy Spirit
during the nineteenth and twentieth centuries. This
outpouring will continue to increase as God fills His
temple, the Body of Christ, with His glory!

The Former Rain

The former rain of God's power fell in former times.
These were the times of the former temple and the former covenants. They were Old Testament times.

Prior to Jesus shedding His blood, a person who died
with faith in the Lord could not go to Heaven. His spirit or
inner man went down to a place called Abraham's Bosom.
It was a place of rest and waiting until Jesus shed His
blood and paid the penalty for the sin of mankind.

The **former rain** that fell during Old Testament
times was **characterized** by the **judgment** of God on
those people who opposed God's plan, His purpose, and
His prophets. Judgment was always **spoken** through
the mouths of God's prophets with the **intent** that those
spoken to should **repent**. If they failed to repent, the
judgment of God would follow. A good example of this is
Moses' speaking to Pharaoh to "Let my people go!"
When Pharaoh refused, God's judgment fell.

This former rain of God's power, which included
great **signs** and **wonders**, is seen throughout the Old

Testament. God used angels to carry out many of these judgments. By the time of the prophet Joel, the former rain **had already** been given.

The Former and Latter Together

JOEL 2:23,24
23 Be glad then, you children of Zion, and rejoice in the Lord your God; for He HAS GIVEN you the FORMER RAIN faithfully, and He will cause the rain to come down for you—the FORMER rain, AND the LATTER rain in the first *month.*
24 The threshing floors shall be full of wheat, and the vats shall overflow with new wine and oil.

This is a picture of the huge harvest at the end of this age. The former rain of God's judgment (hail) falls together with the latter rain of God's mercy (fire) to reap the greatest harvest of souls coming to Jesus in the history of mankind — a harvest so large it cannot be numbered! It is the harvest from the Great Tribulation.

No one living on the earth today has ever experienced the former rain of God. We have never seen angels of God carry out His judgments upon the wicked. We've not seen a "thousand fall at our side and ten thousand at our right hand" (Ps. 91:7). We have never seen the results of a death angel moving throughout the land. Just to think about such things brings many emotions to us. Although our outward man might be glad to see judgment come upon the wicked, it is bitter to the inward man.

As the Body of Christ, we need to understand that the time is swiftly approaching when this former rain of

God's power will start falling, along with the precious sweetness of His latter rain. If we do not understand this, then we will suffer great confusion as to what these judgments are and why they are happening. We must get to the place in God that when they come, we recognize them for what they are — judgments **performed by God**, removing the tares from the harvest fields and answering the voice of the blood of the righteous.

The glory of the latter rain upon those who are truly submitted to the Lord will be so strong that I believe we will recognize His judgments as coming from Him. May we rapidly complete the harvest of the righteous so we can **go home** to our habitation in Heaven!

Chapter XVII

THE TRUMPETS
OF HARVEST

The trumpets of the harvest have been one of the most misunderstood passages of The Revelation of Jesus Christ. The primary reason for this is that they are written, for the most part, in **symbolic language**. Secondly, John is seeing and describing things in Heaven, in the **spiritual realm**, not in the physical realm.

The trumpets of the harvest encompass the **two** final **harvests** of people from the earth. The **first** two trumpets will see a **huge, supernatural harvest** of the **Jews** and the **nations**. Millions, and I believe billions, of people will **come** to **Jesus** during these two trumpets. It will be the loudest cry by the blood of Jesus heard throughout the whole earth. The Gospel will be being preached in **every nation**! God's angels will remove the tares before us as the Holy Spirit brings in the harvest through us, the Church. The Church will walk in the full glory of God, a Church without spot or wrinkle.

The third and fourth trumpet see the harvest diminish as false religion once again attempts to deceive mankind. As the voice of the blood of Jesus becomes muffled by the voice of false religion, then the voice of the blood of the righteous, crying for vengeance upon the wicked, will increase in the throne room of God. The **second** harvest, the **harvest** of the **wicked**, will intensify.

The final three trumpets are **woes**, as God's judgments turn into His wrath. His inward indignation will issue forth in revenge for the blood of His children which was shed for the Word of God and for the testimony of Jesus that they held. The seventh trumpet introduces the seven bowls which complete God's wrath upon the wicked and upon the world system.

REVELATION 8:1-6
1   When He opened the seventh seal, there was silence in heaven for about half an hour.
2   And I saw the seven angels who stand before God, and to them were given SEVEN TRUMPETS.
3   Then another angel, having a golden censer, came and stood at the altar. He was given MUCH INCENSE, that he should offer it with the PRAYERS of ALL THE SAINTS upon the golden altar which was before the throne.
4   And the smoke of the incense, with the prayers of the saints, ascended before God from the angel's hand.
5   Then the angel took the censer, filled it with FIRE from the ALTAR, and threw it to the earth. And there were noises, thunderings, lightnings, and an earthquake.
6   So the seven angels who had the SEVEN TRUMPETS PREPARED themselves TO SOUND.

The seven trumpets are about to sound. What is the reason — the cause — for this event? What propels their action? This event is God's response to much incense and the **prayers** of **all the saints** offered **upon the golden altar before** the **throne** of **Heaven**! What prayers of yours and mine are being placed upon that altar? The prayers that come from our heart, our spirit man, in obedience to His Word and the prompting of His Spirit. The prayers to save mankind, to send laborers into the harvest fields, to preach the Gospel to every creature, to demonstrate His love, to pour out His Spirit, to let His glory cover the earth like the waters cover the sea!

Those prayers are placed upon the same altar that contains the blood of Jesus! And the blood of Jesus is speaking redemption, salvation, deliverance, healing, and restoration!

There is silence in Heaven for half an hour when the seventh seal is opened. Why? Because the seventh seal reveals the seventieth week of Daniel, the final week of this age. This is the time for which everyone in Heaven has been waiting. It is the final great harvest of the earth! It is the time when the Jews and the nations come to Jesus. It is the time when God's family will finally be united forever. It is the time when God will judge the wicked and the world system and avenge the blood of the righteous. It is the **Great Tribulation**. This age is coming to a powerful and swift conclusion. There is silence in Heaven for half an hour. The fire of the Holy Spirit is taken from the altar of God and thrown to the earth, and the last seven years of this age are upon us!

The First Trumpet

"The first angel sounded: And **hail** and **fire** followed, mingled with **blood**, and they were thrown to the **earth**. And a third of the **trees** were burned up, and all green **grass** was burned up" (Rev. 8:7).

We immediately see the two-edged sword of God. **Hail symbolizes** the **judgment** of God, the **former** rain. **Fire symbolizes** the **Holy Spirit**, with His mercy, love, and power — the **latter** rain. They are mingled with the blood of Jesus, the only blood in Heaven, and thrown to the earth. The earth symbolizes Israel. Remember that God is dealing with Israel (the earth) and the nations (the sea), through us, the Church.

Trees represent people — adults — while grass symbolizes children or youth. Green grass is grass that is alive. Symbolically, then, green grass symbolizes spiritually alive children or youth.

So what is the result of this first trumpet? A third of the trees (people) in the earth (Israel) are burned up, and all the green grass (spiritually alive children) are burned up. What are they "burned up" with? The fire of the Holy Spirit! They are **"consumed with"** the fire of the Holy Spirit.

Folks, this is salvation and the infilling with the fire of God, like on the day of Pentecost! They aren't killed; they are saved and filled with the Holy Spirit! God said, "And I will not hide My face from them anymore; for I shall have poured out My Spirit on the house of Israel..." (Ezek. 39:29).

The Second Trumpet

"Then the second angel sounded: And something like a great mountain burning with **fire** was thrown into the **sea**, and a third of the sea became **blood**. And a third of the living creatures in the sea died, and a third of the ships were destroyed" (Rev. 8:8,9).

When the second angel sounds his trumpet, we see a huge outpouring (great mountain) of the Holy Spirit (fire) thrown into the nations (sea) of the earth. The result is one third of the people of the nations (sea) being covered with the blood of Jesus — a huge harvest of souls coming to Jesus from every nation, tribe, tongue, and people!

Because of this huge outpouring of the glory of God into the nations, a third of the living creatures (demonic forces) died (removed by God's angels), and a third of the ships (religions and agencies that perpetuate and carry false doctrine) were destroyed (became ineffective). God's angels remove the tares so we can harvest the wheat!

The Third Trumpet

"Then the third angel sounded: And a great star fell from heaven, burning like a torch, and it fell on a third of the rivers and on the springs of water. The name of the star is Wormwood. A third of the waters became wormwood, and many men died from the water, because it was made bitter" (Rev. 8:10,11).

As it was when Jesus fulfilled His first three and a half years of earthly ministry, so it will be during the last three and a half years of ministry by His Body. The

early part of Jesus' ministry was enormously successful,
but as He entered the latter part of His earthly ministry,
His opposition grew.

The first two trumpets saw a swift, supernatural harvest of Israel and the nations. Now we see entering the
scene a great deceiver, the false prophet (wormwood).
His ministry causes a third of the waters (spiritual life
in the Word of God) to become false. Religion raises its
ugly head, and many men die (spiritually) because of
false teaching.

"For then there will be great tribulation, such as has
not been since the beginning of the world until this time,
no, nor ever shall be. . . . For false christs and false
prophets will rise and show great signs and wonders to
deceive, if possible, even the elect" (Matt. 24:21,24).

Paul said this concerning the coming of our Lord
Jesus Christ and our gathering together to Him.

"Let no one deceive you by any means; for that Day
will not come unless the **falling away** comes **first**. . ."
(II Thess. 2:3).

"From that time many of His disciples went back and
walked with Him no more. Then Jesus said to the
twelve, 'Do you also want to go away?'" (John 6:66,67).

The Fourth Trumpet

"Then the fourth angel sounded: And a third of the
sun was struck, a third of the moon, and a third of the
stars, so that a third of them were darkened. A third of
the day did not shine, and likewise the night" (Rev. 8:12).

With the rise of the false prophet and false religion,

there is less Gospel light. The preaching and teaching of the truth of God's Word becomes a third less effective and shines less brightly because of the rise of false prophets with great signs and wonders.

"And I looked, and I heard an angel flying through the midst of heaven, saying with a loud voice, 'Woe, woe, woe to the inhabitants of the earth, because of the remaining blasts of the trumpet of the three angels who are about to sound!'" (Rev. 8:13).

Woe is an **exclamation of grief**. The angel is exclaiming great grief for the inhabitants of the earth because of the remaining three trumpets. God's judgments now turn into His wrath. As the harvest of the righteous decreases, the harvest of the wicked increases.

God Protects His Children

First of all, it is **very important** that we — you and I — in the Body of Christ realize that we are **not** inhabitants of the earth! Our habitation, our home, is in Heaven. "For our citizenship is in heaven, from which we also eagerly wait for the Savior, the Lord Jesus Christ, who will transform our lowly body that it may be conformed to His glorious body. . ." (Phil. 3:20,21).

We are ambassadors here on earth with full privileges of immunity granted by our Heavenly Father! We have been sealed; our number is 777. We are marked on the forehead, symbolizing that we choose Jesus, and on the right hand, symbolizing our work. We put our hands to the works of God, not to the works of man. We raise our hands to praise and magnify God. Spirit, soul and body, we belong to God!

What we are going to see in the next two trumpets are some severe judgments of God upon the inhabitants of the earth. His judgments and His wrath **do not touch us!**

"They were commanded **not to harm** the grass [children] of the earth, or any green thing [spiritually alive], or any tree [person/adult], but only those men who do not have the seal of God on their foreheads" (Rev. 9:4).

For us to go through this time with peace in our hearts, we must realize that these judgments will not touch us! We have been sealed. We also will be operating in a very strong anointing of the glory of God and with an unprecedented ministry of angels!

Think back to the time when God brought the plagues upon the Egyptians, but those plagues did not touch the Israelites. Even the death angel passed over them because of the blood. Have no fear, folks! You're covered by **the Blood**, sealed by **the Holy Spirit**, and your **habitation** is **in Heaven!**

The Fifth Trumpet (The First Woe)

REVELATION 9:1-6
1   Then the fifth angel sounded: And I saw a star fallen from heaven to the earth. To him was given the key to the bottomless pit.
2   And he opened the bottomless pit, and smoke arose out of the pit like the smoke of a great furnace. So the sun and the air were darkened because of the smoke of the pit.
3   Then out of the smoke locusts came upon the earth. And to them was given power, as the scorpions of the earth have power.
4   They were commanded NOT TO HARM the grass of

the earth, or any green thing, or any tree, but only those men who do not have the seal of God on their foreheads.
5 And they were not given authority to kill them, but to torment them for five months. Their torment was like the torment of a scorpion when it strikes a man.
6 In those days men will seek death and will not find it; they will desire to die, and death will flee from them.

By this time in the harvest, most people who desire to know God will be saved. The judgment (hail) edge of God's sword becomes increasingly active. God sends an angel (star) from Heaven to release evil spirits (locusts) from the bottomless pit.

It is important to understand that God has all authority in Heaven, in earth, and under the earth! God places evil spirits in the bottomless pit, and God releases evil spirits. The devil is not in control of the compartments of Hades; God has that authority! The devil and his demons are confined to the atmosphere around the earth. That is their prison for a few more years until they also are confined to the bottomless pit.

During this fifth trumpet, a period of about five months, God releases evil spirits from that bottomless pit to torment men and women who are not sealed by God. Our outward man might like what is happening to them, but our inward man will be grieved.

The Sixth Trumpet (The Second Woe)

REVELATION 9:13-16
13 Then the sixth angel sounded: And I heard a voice from the four horns of the golden altar which is before God,

14 saying to the sixth angel who had the trumpet, "Release the four angels who are bound at the great river Euphrates."
15 So the four angels, who had been prepared for the hour and day and month and year, were released to kill a third of mankind.
16 Now the number of the army of the horsemen was two hundred million; I heard the number of them.

It is important to see that **God is doing this!** As I read the description of this army that is with the four angels, I am convinced it is a spiritual army, an army of spirit beings, not a natural army of men. Just as the death angel went throughout Egypt, so these four angels and their army will go throughout the earth and kill a third of mankind!

Keep in mind as you study the Book of The Revelation of Jesus Christ that the Apostle John was caught up to Heaven. He is seeing and describing things that are happening in the **spiritual realm.**

We must now remember that the two witnesses and the completed Body of Christ are ministering in great power and authority throughout these first six trumpets. They will prophesy 1,260 days, standing before the god of the earth. They have power to shut heaven so that no rain falls. They have power over waters to turn them to blood. They have power to strike the earth with **all plagues,** as often as they desire!

The plagues that we see in these last trumpets are in response to the words of prophecy, the fire of the Holy Spirit, that proceeds out of the mouths of His prophets.

God will speak through the mouths of His servants in His body, and He will perform His words! God will call down upon the evil men of the earth, through the mouths of His prophets, the plagues of judgment (former rain).

REVELATION 9:20,21
20 But the rest of mankind, who were not killed by these plagues, DID NOT REPENT of the works of their hands, that they should not worship demons, and idols of gold, silver, brass, stone, and wood, which can neither see nor hear nor walk.
21 And they DID NOT REPENT of their murders or their sorceries or their sexual immorality or their thefts.

What this is describing is the time in history when there are no more people on the face of the earth who will receive Jesus. Only hardened hearts are left who refuse and reject the light of God's Word. The six trumpets of harvest are complete, and every creature has heard and seen the Gospel. God has a family in the earth that encompasses every nation, tribe, people, and tongue.

His Church and His prophets have completed the Great Commission to, "...Go into all the world and preach the gospel to every creature. He who believes and is baptized will be saved; but he who does not believe **will be condemned**" (Mark 16:15,16).

The two witnesses surrender their lives over to death, but God's family from the nations, tribes, peoples, and tongues will not allow them to be buried!

Why? Because we know what is going to happen in three and a half days! For three and a half days, the people of the earth rejoice, because they had been tormented by the prophets of God.

But then, ". . .the breath of life from God entered them, and they stood on their feet, and great fear fell on those who saw them. And they heard a loud voice from heaven saying to them, '**Come up here**.' And they ascended to heaven in a cloud, and their enemies saw them" (Rev. 11:11,12).

"But in the days of the sounding of the seventh angel, when he is **about** to sound, the **mystery** of **God** would be **finished**, as He declared to His servants the prophets" (Rev. 10:7).

REVELATION 11:13-15
13 In the same hour there was a great earthquake, and a tenth of the city fell. In the earthquake seven thousand people were killed, and the rest were afraid and gave glory to the God of heaven.
14 The second woe is past. Behold, the third woe is coming quickly.
15 Then the seventh angel sounded. . . .

Chapter XVIII

GOD'S WRATH COMPLETED

Then the seventh angel sounded [the **third woe**]:
*And there were loud voices in heaven, saying, "The
kingdoms of this world have become the kingdoms of
our Lord and of His Christ, and He shall reign forever
and ever!"...*

*Then the temple of God was opened in heaven, and
the ark of His covenant was seen in His temple. And
there were lightnings, noises, thunderings, an earthquake, and **great hail**.*

— Revelation 11:15,19

Just as hail symbolizes judgment, great hail symbolizes the completion of the wrath of God. The seventh
trumpet introduces the seven bowls of God's wrath.
During this final period of the Great Tribulation, God's
people will have been taken off the earth to their home
in Heaven. The Holy Spirit will still be on the earth, so
people can be saved. It will be the most horrible time in
human history.

Spirit of Antichrist

The people on the earth will come under the sway of
the spirit of antichrist. "Anti" means *against* and
"Christ" means *anointed of God*. The spirit of antichrist
is resident in religion. It cannot stand the anointing or

power of God. Religion and the spirit of antichrist "gnash their teeth" at the signs, wonders, and miracles of the Holy Spirit. They blaspheme the work of the Holy Spirit. It was the Holy Spirit who anointed Jesus, and it is the Holy Spirit who anoints the members of His Body, the Church. The spirit of antichrist cannot dominate until we, the Church, are taken home.

We are the salt and light of the world. It is God, working through us, that restrains evil.

II THESSALONIANS 2:7,8
7   For the mystery of lawlessness is already at work; only He who now restrains will do so until He is taken out of the way.
8   And then the lawless one will be revealed, whom the Lord will consume with the breath of His mouth and destroy with the brightness of His coming.

God will pour out His wrath in response to the voice of the blood of His children which cries from within the earth. It cries to Him for justice and vengeance upon those who dwell upon the earth.

Mystery Babylon

As God pours out His wrath, He will judge Mystery Babylon the Great, mother of harlots and of the abominations of the earth.

A harlot is one who makes herself attractive and exposes herself to attract men away from their intended lover. All mankind was designed to receive the love of God and to fall in love with Jesus. However, the **world**

system, the cosmos, **of which Satan is god,** is dressed up and perfumed and exposed to entice men away from God. Its primary focus is the lust for money and power. It is clothed and perfumed in materialism, commerce, financial empires, arts, religions, and asceticism.

"Asceticism" is denying self to do good *deeds*, as opposed to *divine good*. People devote their whole lives to projects, which they believe are good, without seeking to know God's will in the matter and allowing *Him* to direct their paths. They are trying to justify themselves by their own good deeds. Although their efforts may be for worthy causes, but such deeds that are neither initiated or directed by the Holy Spirit will eventually be consumed by fire. This world system — this Mystery Babylon, this mother of harlots — will receive the wrath of God because the **blood** of His **servants** is **found in her,** and she **deceived all** the **nations.**

REVELATION 15:1
1 Then I saw another sign in heaven, great and marvelous: seven angels having the seven last plagues, for in them the WRATH of God is complete.

REVELATION 16:2-6,17-19
2 So the first went and poured out his bowl upon the EARTH, and a foul and loathsome sore came upon the MEN who HAD the MARK of the BEAST and those who worshiped his image.
3 Then the second angel poured out his bowl on the SEA, and it became blood as of a dead man; and every living creature in the sea died.
4 Then the third angel poured out his bowl on the rivers and springs of water, and they became blood.

5   And I heard the angel of the waters saying: "You are righteous, O Lord, the One who is and who was and who is to be, because You have judged these things.
6   For THEY have SHED the BLOOD of SAINTS AND PROPHETS, and You have given them blood to drink. For it is their just due. . . ."
17 Then the seventh angel poured out his bowl into the air, and a loud voice came out of the temple of heaven, from the throne, saying, "It is done!"
18 And there were noises and thunderings and lightnings; and there was a great earthquake, such a mighty and great earthquake as has not occurred since men were on the earth.
19 Now the great city divided into three parts, and the cities of the nations fell. And great Babylon was remembered before God, to give her the cup of the wine of the fierceness of His wrath.

REVELATION 18:21,23,24
21 Then a mighty angel took up a stone like a great millstone and threw it into the sea, saying, "Thus with violence the great city Babylon shall be thrown down, and shall not be found anymore. . . .
23 ". . . For your merchants were the great men of the earth, for by YOUR SORCERY ALL the NATIONS were DECEIVED.
24 "And IN HER was FOUND the BLOOD of PROPHETS and SAINTS, and of ALL who were SLAIN on the EARTH."

REVELATION 19:1,2
1   After these things I heard a loud voice of a great multitude in heaven, saying, "Alleluia! Salvation and glory and honor and power belong to the Lord our God!
2   "For true and righteous are His judgments, because He has judged the great harlot who corrupted the

earth with her fornication; and HE has AVENGED on her the BLOOD of His servants shed by her."

Chapter XIX

HIS SECOND COMING

After this great judgment by God, we see in Heaven the call to the Marriage Supper of the Lamb. Those fellow servants, who through their righteous acts received a **fine linen** garment, will be called to the Marriage Supper of the Lamb. They will return to this earth and rule and reign with Jesus during the next age. Those who served Him well here on earth in their natural bodies will return with Him in their glorified bodies to serve Him during a thousand-year period on this earth. Revelation 19:7-16 describes the event in this manner:

REVELATION 19:7-16
7 "Let us be glad and rejoice and give Him glory, for the marriage of the Lamb has come, and His wife has made herself ready."
8 And to her it was granted to be arrayed in fine linen, clean and bright, for the FINE LINEN is the RIGHTEOUS ACTS OF THE SAINTS.
9 Then he said to me, "Write: 'Blessed are those who are called to the marriage supper of the Lamb!'" And he said to me, "These are the true sayings of God."
10 And I fell at his feet to worship him. But he said to me, "See that you do not do that! I am your fellow servant, and of your brethren who have the testimony of Jesus. Worship God! For the testimony of Jesus is the spirit of prophecy."

11 Now I saw heaven opened, and behold, a white horse. And He who sat on him was called Faithful and True, and in righteousness He judges and makes war.
12 His eyes were like a flame of fire, and on His head were many crowns. He had a name written that no one knew except Himself.
13 He was clothed with a robe dipped in blood, and His name is called The Word of God.
14 And the armies in heaven, clothed in FINE LINEN, white and clean, followed Him on white horses.
15 Now out of His mouth goes a sharp sword, that with it He should strike the nations. And He Himself will rule them with a rod of iron. He Himself treads the winepress of the fierceness and wrath of Almighty God.
16 And He has on His robe and on His thigh a name written:

King of kings
And Lord of lords!

Jesus' first coming to earth was as the Lamb of God, to take away the sin of the world. His second coming to this earth will be as King of kings and Lord of lords. He will destroy His enemies with the words of His mouth and establish His reign upon the earth. Every knee shall bow, and every tongue confess, that Jesus Christ is Lord (Phil. 2:10,11)!

Conclusion

The time is short, and the harvest fields are huge. God is raising up, equipping, and sending forth His harvesters over all the earth. He is cleansing every hungry heart with the fire of the Holy Spirit.

As we move closer and closer to the end of the age, the distinction between light and darkness, good and evil, will grow ever sharper. The Church will increase in spiritual power and anointing as God's glory fills His temple. As we harvest the wheat by the indwelling presence of God, His angels will remove the tares from the fields before us. Many angels (symbolized as stars in the Book of Revelation) will come from Heaven to earth in these last years, some of which have been prepared for this very hour, day, month and year.

When the last two prophets give up their lives in Jerusalem, look up, the **redemption** of **your body** is only three and a half days away! Then, the **mystery of God** will be **finished**!